Race, Ethnicity, and Disability

Using data from more than 40,000 soldiers of the Union army, this book focuses on the experience of African Americans and immigrants with disabilities, investigating their decision to seek government assistance and their resulting treatment. Pension administrators treated these ex-soldiers differently from native-born whites, but the discrimination was far from seamless – biased evaluations of worthiness intensified in response to administrators' workload and nativists' late-nineteenth-century campaigns. This book finds a remarkable interplay of social concepts, historical context, bureaucratic expediency, and individual initiative. Examining how African Americans and immigrants weighed their circumstances in deciding when to request a pension, employ a pension attorney, or seek institutionalization, it contends that these veterans quietly asserted their right to benefits. Shedding new light on the long history of challenges faced by veterans with disabilities, the book underscores the persistence of these challenges in spite of the recent revolution in disability rights.

Larry M. Logue is Professor of History and Political Science at Mississippi College. He won the Francis and Emily Chipman First-Book Prize for *A Sermon in the Desert: Belief and Behavior in Early St. George, Utah*, and is the author of *To Appomattox and Beyond: The Civil War Soldier in War and Peace* and co-editor of *The Civil War Soldier: A Historical Reader* and *The Civil War Veteran: A Historical Reader*.

Peter Blanck is a University Professor at Syracuse University and Chairman of the Burton Blatt Institute (BBI). He is a trustee of YAI/National Institute for People with Disabilities Network and Chairman of the Global Universal Design Commission (GUDC). Blanck's most recent book is *Disability Civil Rights Law and Policy* (with Hill, Siegal, and Waterstone).

DISABILITY, LAW AND POLICY SERIES

The Disability, Law and Policy series examines these topics in interdisciplinary and comparative terms. The books in the series reflect the diversity of definitions, causes, and consequences of discrimination against persons with disabilities, while illuminating fundamental themes that unite countries in their pursuit of human rights laws and policies to improve the social and economic status of persons with disabilities. The series contains historical, contemporary, and comparative scholarship crucial to identifying individual, organizational, cultural, attitudinal, and legal themes necessary for the advancement of disability law and policy.

The book topics covered in the series also are reflective of the new moral and political commitment by countries throughout the world toward equal opportunity for persons with disabilities in such areas as employment, housing, transportation, rehabilitation, and individual human rights. The series will thus play a significant role in informing policy makers, researchers, and citizens of issues central to disability rights and disability antidiscrimination policies. The series grounds the future of disability law and policy as a vehicle for ensuring that those living with disabilities participate as equal citizens of the world.

Race, Ethnicity, and Disability

Veterans and Benefits in Post-Civil War America

LARRY M. LOGUE

PETER BLANCK

CAMBRIDGE
UNIVERSITY PRESS

CAMBRIDGE UNIVERSITY PRESS
Cambridge, New York, Melbourne, Madrid, Cape Town,
Singapore, São Paulo, Delhi, Mexico City

Cambridge University Press
32 Avenue of the Americas, New York NY 10013-2473, USA

Published in the United States of America by Cambridge University Press, New York

www.cambridge.org
Information on this title: www.cambridge.org/9781107610583

First published 2010
First paperback edition 2013

A catalogue record for this publication is available from the British Library

Library of Congress Cataloging in Publication data
Logue, Larry M., 1947–
Race, ethnicity, and disability : veterans and benefi ts in post–Civil War
America / Larry M. Logue, Peter Blanck.
p. cm. – (Disability, law and policy series)
Includes bibliographical references and index.
ISBN 978-0-521-51634-1 (hardback)
1. United States – History – Civil War, 1861–1865 – Veterans –
Pensions. 2. Disabled veterans – Pensions – United States – History –
19th century. 3. African American veterans – Pensions – History – 19th
century. 4. Military pensions – United States – Civil War, 1861–1865.
5. Racism – United States – History – 19th century. 6. United States – Race
relations – History –19th century. 7. Immigrants – United States – Social
conditions – 19th century. 8. Veterans – United States – Social conditions –
19th century. 9. United States. Army – Minorities – History – 19th
century. I. Blanck, Peter David, 1957– II. Title. III. Series.
UB373.L64 2010
331.25′2913550097309034 – dc22   2010004172

ISBN 978-0-521-51634-1 Hardback
ISBN 978-1-107-61058-3 Paperback

Contents

Contents

Tables and Figure

Tables

Tables and Figure

Tables and Figure

Figure

Illustrations

Abbreviated Citations in Notes

CR	U.S. Congress, *Congressional Record*
Managers Report	Board of Managers of National Home for Disabled Volunteer Soldiers, *Annual Reports*
MPM Records	Robert W. Fogel et al., *Aging of Veterans of the Union Army: Military, Pension, and Medical Records, 1820–1940*
OR	U.S. War Department, *War of the Rebellion: A Compilation of the Official Records of the Union and Confederate Armies, 1861–1865*

Abbreviated Citations in Notes

Pension Files	Pension Files, 1861–1934, National Archives, Washington, D.C.
Report of Commissioner	U.S. Department of Interior, Bureau of Pensions, *Reports of Commissioner of Pensions*
SL	U.S. Congress, *U.S. Statutes at Large*
Surgeons' Certificates	Robert W. Fogel et al., *Aging of Veterans of the Union Army: Surgeons' Certificates, Version S-1 Standardized, 1862–1940*

Foreword

The promise of America advanced closer to reality when the Americans with Disabilities Act was signed into law by President George H. W. Bush in 1990. As attorney general at the time and the parent of a son with physical and intellectual disability, I knew that the law was necessary because people with disabilities had been forced into the shadows of the legal system, denied basic protections against being seen and treated as "second-class citizens."

While advocates of the ADA were lobbying for improved opportunities, other Americans with disabilities had long been eligible for government assistance meant to improve their quality of life. This aid began with pensions for former soldiers of the Revolutionary War, was later supplemented by assisted living in soldiers' homes, and came in the twentieth century to include rehabilitation of veterans with disabilities. What does the experience of this discrete group tell us about the role of disability in American society?

This book looks closely at how benefits were awarded to the men who fought for the North in the Civil War. Professors Logue and Blanck find that the federal government's sympathy for people with disabilities came at the price of judgment calls about some veterans' worthiness. Missing arms and legs were easy enough to verify, but a man with back pain might be suspected of faking, and another man's headaches might be due to "vicious habits" like alcoholism. The government officials who made these judgments needed some basis upon which to proceed, especially when the applications began to pile up in the thousands and then the hundreds of thousands. Race was an easy and unfortunate basis for a snap judgment, and when some classes of immigrants were labeled as racially inferior near the turn of the twentieth century, their credibility came to be mistrusted too. Professors Logue and Blanck make a thorough investigation of these kinds of discrimination in the Civil War benefits system.

Racial and ethnic discrimination in benefits for Civil War veterans should concern those who oversee today's benefits for veterans, because the current system seems to rely on many of the same principles. It should also concern those involved in the struggle for equal rights under the ADA. Though the ADA is not about monetary benefits, some of those who challenge its implementation make accusations of "gaming the system" that echo critics of nineteenth-century veterans.

Logue and Blanck alert those who care about rights for people with disabilities to be ever mindful of the motivations that may underlie government actions.

Dick Thornburgh

Acknowledgments

This book has acquired a number of benefactors. Larry Logue is grateful to Mississippi College for providing a sabbatical leave during the initial phase of the project and travel funds later on, and to the Burton Blatt Institute (BBI) of Syracuse University for a fellowship at a crucial stage.

Peter Blanck is thankful to colleagues at the Burton Blatt Institute and the Syracuse College of Law at Syracuse University, as well as to numerous colleagues around the globe who listened to colloquia and provided feedback on this program of investigation.

This project was funded in part by grants to Peter Blanck and BBI from: (a) the National Institute on Disability and Rehabilitation Research (NIDRR), U.S. Department of Education, as follows – (i) "Demand Side

Employment Placement Models," Grant No. H133A060033; (ii) "The Asset Accumulation and Economic Self-Sufficiency Project," Grant No. H133A090014; (iii) "Southeast Disability & Business Technical Assistance Center," Grant No. H133A060094; and (iv) "Center on Effective Delivery of Rehabilitation Technology by Vocational Rehabilitation Agencies," Grant No. H133A090004; (b) the Rehabilitation Services Administration (RSA) for the "Southeast Region TACE Center," Grant No. H264A080021; and (c) the Office of Disability Employment Policy (ODEP), U.S. Department of Labor, "Disability Case Study Research Consortium," Grant/Contract #E-9-4-6-0107.

The authors gratefully acknowledge the support of NIH/ NIA grant number P01 AG10120, Early Indicators of Later Work Levels, Disease and Death – Robert W. Fogel, principal investigator. We are indebted to Noelle Yetter and Alex Gendlin of the University of Chicago's Center for Population Economics for assistance with pension documents and the CPE database. At BBI, William N. Myhill, James Schmeling, Elizabeth Ribet, Sofiya Aramova, Kenneth Hunt, Erica Dolak, and Jeffrey Davenport provided invaluable help in manuscript preparation.

And then there are those debts that thanks can't quite cover. Barbara Logue was again an incisive reviewer, forbearing listener, sage counselor, and so much more. Wendy Blanck as always is in the so much more category, along with Jason, Daniel, Albert, Caroline, and Harry.

Introduction

This is an investigation of a public policy's effects on the people who encountered it. It is customary to frame such studies within analyses of partisan politics and interest groups, and we will attend to these subjects. We are primarily concerned, however, with the impact of ideas on experience.

One cornerstone of this book is an analysis of the disabilities presented by veterans of the Union army as they negotiated the federal government's system of military benefits. This cornerstone, comprising tangible evidence such as amputations and hospital confinements, would appear to have little to do with any form of ideas, but the reverse is true.

Benefits for Civil War veterans were primarily shaped by American society's dominant attitude toward disability, which has been termed the "medical model." In this conception, which persists today, disabling conditions signify deviation from "normality," and the first obligation of the worthy individual with a disability is to obtain a "cure" or rehabilitation. Discussions of this paradigm typically locate its origins in the rise of the modern concept of normality and in the medical profession's crusade for respectability, both of which took place in the nineteenth century. Common parlance, however, indicates a longer history of identifying individuals by their disabilities: "deaf," "blind," "cripple," and "lunatic" were used as nouns well before the nineteenth century, implicitly employing the medical model's equation of personhood and disability.[1]

The alternative understanding of disability has been called the "social" (or "rights-based") model, which redirects attention from the individual and his or her disabilities to the medical model's intolerance of them. Viewed in this way, disability is essentially the product of society's preoccupation with "normality." In a host of ways, from viewing impairments as defects to restricting public policies and physical facilities to the "able-bodied," "normal" society has employed the medical model to turn *disability* into *inability*; it is society that should be rehabilitated, not just the individual. Although this study is about the effects rather than the formation of public policies, we point out ways in which disability models informed policies on veterans' benefits.[2]

Perceptions have affected Americans' experience of disability in another way. Scholars have likened disabilities to stigmata, focusing on the strategies adopted by individuals to cope with social and institutional reactions to a disabling condition. Because virtually all empirical studies of the subject have focused on our own time, there is considerable scope for exploring stigmatization in the past.[3]

Military benefits may appear to be an ill-fitting framework for studying stigmatization. Much of the strategy for coping with stigmatized conditions consists of concealment to pass for "normal," yet applicants for military benefits were required to make public presentation of potentially stigmatizing disabilities. Because it offered compensation to those who "sacrificed health, competence, ... and the certainties of a comfortable old age, all for the sake of battling for the old flag and the perpetuity of republican institutions," the federal government seemed to view veterans' disabilities not as signs of "shameful differentness" but as "prestige symbols."[4]

Nonetheless, exploration of these benefits offers unique opportunities for assessing stigmatization of people with disabilities. We cannot assume that veterans always understood their own disabilities as prestige symbols. For example, though most amputees in a penmanship competition described their wounds as "honorable scars," one veteran admitted that "to be a permanent cripple for life" meant losing "our place in society," and another wrote that he "might as well be black." And if a missing arm did signify patriotic sacrifice, what about chronic diarrhea resulting from army food, or a former prisoner of war's "spells of melancholy"? Disabling conditions were not necessarily equivalent, and

Private Samuel H. Decker, 9th U.S. Artillery, and his "honorable scars." (Library of Congress)

we therefore examine patterns in the presentation of disabilities and official responses to them as clues to veterans' attitude toward their disabilities.[5]

This investigation's second cornerstone offers another reason to investigate stigmatization. Analysts acknowledge

RESULT OF APPOINTING A VETERAN AS POSTMASTER.

"Result of Appointing a Veteran as Postmaster." Not everyone saw veterans' disabilities as "prestige symbols." Cartoon from *Frank Leslie's Illustrated Newspaper*, Feb. 11, 1865. (Musselman Library, Gettysburg College)

that membership in a racial or ethnic group can itself constitute a stigma, thereby compounding the effects of disability. An African-American penmanship competitor, for example, wrote that "I don[']t expect to secure a position as *clerk*, that being proscribed on account of my *color*." Because this book is concerned with the implications of race and ethnicity in the veterans' benefits system, we also search for distinctive responses to being an African American or an immigrant *and* having a disability.[6]

We have chosen race and ethnicity as our second cornerstone because these were especially potent ideas in post–Civil War America. Convictions about essential differences between whites and other races inevitably extended to the veterans' benefits system. African Americans who applied for a pension or admission to a soldiers' home brought perceived differences to the forefront; likewise, applicants with names such as Colobarzo or Gapczenski, though they had lived in America for decades, were reminders of a gathering threat to the nation's "racial integrity." We examine the experience of African Americans and immigrants in the Civil War benefits system, to identify tangible consequences of friction between whites and "other" groups.

Proceeding from these cornerstones, this book concentrates on administration rather than formulation of policies on veterans' benefits for two reasons. First, a number of thorough studies have traced the rise and development of benefits for Civil War veterans. Second, a focus on race and ethnicity finds little to examine in veterans' policy creation. Laws and regulations regarding veterans' benefits dwell on documenting military service and ascertaining disabilities rather than on beneficiaries' characteristics; the policies are on their face largely race neutral.[7]

This de jure neutrality did not perforce extend to policy administration. The Pension Bureau employed its own army of reviewers, referees, and clerks, yet it was part of a federal bureaucracy that was only beginning to evolve into a fourth branch of government. Functioning primarily as a clerical workforce, executive-branch agencies had developed mere rudiments of the expertise and independent authority needed to plan, manage, and regulate the activities of a national state.[8]

The Pension Bureau occupied a complex place in this evolution. On the one hand, the Bureau's complement was largely clerical, with employment based on veteran preference: as late as 1904, though it had developed a middle-management cadre of deputies and chiefs, more than three-quarters of the Bureau's 1,690 workers were clerks, and one-quarter of all employees were veterans (supplemented by ex-soldiers' survivors, who also received hiring preference). Moreover, in Chapter 2 we acknowledge Congressional intervention in decision making and the Bureau's failure to gain direct control over physical examinations for pensions.[9]

Yet we also argue that the Pension Bureau strove to carve out a discretionary authority in the face of powerful outside forces such as veterans' organizations and pension attorneys. The Bureau attempted to impose order on an unruly benefits system by reviewing all and rejecting some pension applications, including many that had been tailored by pension attorneys' "claim houses" and endorsed by examining physicians. Patterns in these rejections, especially those reflecting applicants' race or ethnicity, are telltale signs of these attempts at order; we highlight such patterns and discuss their consequences for the nature of subsequent social-insurance programs and more recent shifts in attitudes and laws regarding disability.

We have also limited our empirical investigation to benefits for Civil War veterans themselves. The Union army pension system actually comprised multiple programs, one for veterans and others for their widows, children, and dependent parents. This book focuses on race and ethnicity in a system of *disability* benefits; dependents participated in programs of *survivors'* benefits, with their own premises and procedures. The latter programs have begun to receive the scholarly attention that is warranted by their distinctive character.[10]

Though this study centers on race, ethnicity, and social perceptions of disability, we adduce other concepts such as assumptions about masculinity to assist in understanding veterans' reactions to their treatment by government officials. We hasten to add that this is not a brief for cultural determinism, and we will give other forces their due as our sources permit. We seek above all a balanced analysis of the circumstances that shaped veterans' experience with a public program, the influences on their response to this experience, and the implications of the experience and the response for the development of public policies down to our own time.

1

The Winding Path of the Self and the Other

Just as formal disciplines have terms for relationships – the plus sign, the conjunction, and the like –
everyday life has its own relational terms, including
race, ethnicity, and disability. These concepts do more than
classify people: they delineate one's own group as well as
"other" groups, and they specify relationships of status
and power among those they categorize. Such concepts are
meant to convey fundamental truths that lend coherence to
an otherwise bewildering world of human behavior.

Unlike the formal relational terms, however, race,
ethnicity, and disability are far from fixed or universal.
Historians have pointed to the malleability of race and
similar concepts – they fluctuate not only over time, but
also among groups and places. To take only one example,
skin color, the reflexive signifier of race, was relatively

unimportant in late-nineteenth-century African Americans' appraisal of whites. Indeed, a recent assertion about gender applies equally to other relational concepts: gender categories are simultaneously empty and overfilled, meaning that they lack tangible referents yet encompass a host of understandings and assumptions, some compatible and some contradictory. A key achievement of recent scholarship is its demonstration that the formation and functioning of race and related inventions must be investigated rather than assumed.[1]

This book focuses on the role of race and ethnicity in a federal program designed to assist veterans of the Union armed forces. The task for this chapter then is to sketch the contours of the key concepts as they stood in the late nineteenth and early twentieth centuries; doing so will set the stage for the exploration of the Civil War pension system in Chapter 2.

Beneath the shifting sands of racial and ethnic distinctions in the Gilded Age lay the more stable notion of "self-government." Matthew Frye Jacobson makes the insightful observation that the naturalization law of 1790, which opened the way to citizenship for "free white" immigrants, rested on an equation of race and responsibility. White men (with white women presumably exerting influence as wives and mothers) were deemed capable of governing their passions, and they could be full members of "the people" who held ultimate authority in a republic; people of color, allegedly susceptible to emotion and impulse, were judged unfit to be republican stakeholders. A Pennsylvania politician thus declared in 1837 that "I use the word citizen as not embracing the coloured population," and Stephen A. Douglas insisted that the founders meant "no reference either to the negro, the savage Indians, the Fejee, the Malay, or any other inferior and degraded race, when they spoke of the equality of men."[2]

This insistence on a racial basis for genuine citizenship survived Reconstruction-era efforts to extend political and civil rights to African Americans. Writing in 1896, an influential statistician argued that "political liberties, granted with disregard for natural inequalities or stages of human progress, must affect injuriously, in the end, the race on which they were thus conferred." In the writer's view, "The Aryan race is possessed of all the essential characteristics that make for success in the struggle for the higher life," especially "self reliance in man and chastity in woman," while African Americans languished in "increasing immorality, criminality and pauperism."[3]

It is easy to see how the concept of self-government could also be applied to people with disabilities, though what was at stake was usually not citizenship but rather institutional care and a potential "cure" for their condition. In the early nineteenth century, mental illness, for example, was believed to have a double connection to self-government – mental illness not only *produced* inability to govern the self, but was thought to *originate* in "luxury, self-indulgence, sensuality, and effeminacy." Insane asylums, by imposing order and discipline, were supposed to cure the malady.

Likewise, experts believed that deafness reduced people "to the level of mere animal life," which might be remedied by teaching sign language.[4]

The decades after the Civil War saw a substantial reordering of ideas about race, ethnicity, and disability. The causes were many and varied: perceived threats to white supremacy in the South, originating in fears of a second Reconstruction and fueled by white women's doubts about their men's efficacy; burgeoning industries' need for workers and the related influx of immigrants, especially from southern and eastern Europe; and a rising fascination with scientific investigation and its apparent ability to penetrate the unknown.

The consequences of these developments were likewise varied. In the South, whites' suspicion of African Americans hardened into paranoia, resulting in the 1890s in disfranchisement of African Americans, legalized segregation, and an epidemic of lynching. Elsewhere, science seemed to offer an ideal response to the bewildering multiplicity of immigrants. The traditional racial dichotomy of white and not-white was rendered obsolete by steadily increasing references to "physical types" and "stocks," based on authoritative analyses of human appearance and behavior. Whiteness was now subdivided into "races": members of the superior race were variously identified as Anglo-Saxons, Caucasians, Nordics, or Aryans, with their alleged inferiors labeled as Celts, Slavs, Semites, Italics, and so on, depending on who did the labeling.[5]

Even as identified races multiplied, "self-government" remained a cornerstone of racial thinking. Anglo-Saxons, wrote a leading economist, "take up readily and easily the problems of self-care and self-government," whereas immigrants from southern and eastern Europe had "no inherited instincts of self-government [and know] no restraint upon their own passions but the club of the policemen or the bayonet of the soldier." Such convictions led to the formation of the short-lived American Protective Association and the more potent Immigration Restriction League. Bolstered by the eugenics movement's dread of "race suicide," the fear of immigrants culminated in the 1920s in legislation restricting entry to the United States.[6]

The idea of self-government is equally visible at the intersection of immigration policy and disability. As multiple classifications of whites became increasingly accepted, so did the division of immigrants into those who were "normal" and those who were "defective." Beginning in the early 1880s, Congress authorized, and immigration officials delineated, physical and mental conditions to disqualify some new arrivals from admission to the United States; the stated purpose of the policy was to guard against new residents who were "likely to become a public charge." Armed with this authority and influenced by concurrent efforts to ban "unsightly or disgusting" people from public spaces, immigration officials developed an image of the "defective" person who was allegedly unable to care for him- or herself, and by implication, the "normal" person who was self-sufficient: defective people had asthma or heart disease, were "deficient in muscular development," or had curvature of the spine, among a host of other conditions. Evidence of past self-reliance was largely irrelevant; the key distinction between normality and abnormality was the evidence of the inspector's eyes.[7]

It would be a mistake to end discussion of these relational concepts here, because they never quite achieved the unassailable stature their advocates envisioned. Members of the "inferior" groups developed their own explanations of social relationships: African-American writers, for example, insisted that "there is nothing in race or blood, in the color of our features that imparts susceptibility of improvement to one race over another," yet no people "are so domineering, none have a stronger and more exclusive sense of caste; none have a more contemptuous dislike of inferiority" than did whites.[8]

Denouncing national quotas in the landmark Immigration Act of 1924, a rabbi derided "the Nordic" as a "non-existant race ... devised to prove its [own] superiority and in order to prove the inferiority of some of the great races of the earth which are unacceptable to the inventors of the Nordic." In a similar vein, the essayist Randolph Bourne wrote an extended critique of exclusionism based on disability. Affected by conditions including malformed facial features and curvature of the spine, Bourne recognized that an individual with disabilities "is discounted at the start." The fundamental problem was that we "get our ideas and standards of worth from the successful, without reflecting that the interpretations of life which patriotic legend, copy-book philosophy, and the sayings of the wealthy give us, are pitifully inadequate for those who fall behind in the race."[9]

Taken together, these critiques make up a logically consistent alternative to the dominant theories of race, ethnicity, and disability. Long before the argument was widely accepted among scholars, members of "inferior" groups insisted that the equating of visible attributes and character was a fabrication. In making this case, African Americans, ethnic groups, and people with disabilities were asserting that those in power, however they managed to acquire it, had sought out their common features and forged them into conceptual tools such as race and physical "normality" in order to *keep* power.

According to this dissenting theory of society, people should be evaluated by what they *did* rather than what they *were*, so it was a theory rooted in action; yet it provided few guidelines for those who hoped for dignified lives in the face of prevailing convictions that race and physical soundness were destiny. To be sure, there were various tactics available for getting along: African Americans and people with disabilities could modify their aspirations, as advised by Booker T. Washington and Randolph Bourne, and immigrants could emulate "older" groups or distance themselves from African Americans by adopting racist attitudes and behavior.[10]

None of these tactics, however, responded to a fundamental theme in the dominant and dissenting discourses on race, ethnicity, and disability. Self-government was intertwined with assumptions about manhood: the dominant view of social relationships held that the same discipline that underlay self-government also supported manhood, and that these traits were unevenly distributed among the population.[11]

Men of color were a special target for denigration. The organizers of the World's Columbian Exposition of 1893, for example, juxtaposed the majestic White City with the lewd dancing of a "Dahomey gentleman, (or perhaps it is a Dahomey lady, for the distinction is not obvious)"; African Americans recognized the equation of self-government with manhood when they perceived, as did Ida B. Wells, that "having destroyed the citizenship of the man, [whites with their campaign of disfranchisement and segregation] are now trying to destroy the manhood of the citizen."[12]

As whiteness came to be subdivided, critics likewise disparaged the manliness of "inferior" whites. One writer reported being told that "you can't make boy scouts out of the Jews," and that "they are absolute babies about pain. Their young fellows will scream with a hard lick." This disdain extended beyond Jews: the same writer concluded that, in contrast to the typical manly traits of "discipline, sense of duty, presence of mind, and consideration for the weak" that were evident among northern Europeans, southern Europeans were "limited by selfishness and bad faith."[13]

Denying the manliness of those with disabilities has a long history, epitomized by English poor law's label of "impotent" for those who were not "able-bodied." This prejudice was apparently increasing in Gilded-Age America: pressured by rising competition for jobs, railroad workers who had once admired the fortitude of injured trainmen, for example, began to question the diligence and competence, and hence the manliness, of co-workers who had become disabled.[14]

Yet these assaults on manhood also pointed to a course of action. Because manliness was achieved as well as ascribed, men from "inferior" backgrounds could defy expectations, prove their manliness, and hope to sever the assumed link between background and character. Enlisting in the Civil War was an ideal way to offer this proof. African Americans were especially likely to insist on the connection of service to manliness: one soldier recalled that he "felt like a man with a uniform on and a gun in my hand," and another declared that "now t[h]ings can never go back, because we have showed our energy and our courage and our [natural] manhood." After the War, veterans could reaffirm their manly devotion by claiming a federal pension.[15]

It might seem that a study of pensions would shed little light on the experience of disability in the Gilded Age, because policies of inclusion apparently had little in common with the exclusionism faced by civilians with disabilities. To dismiss pensions as an anomaly, however, would be to overlook an arena in which the forces that shaped Americans' experiences with disability were expressed and contested.

Pensions, in general, fit somewhere between the medical and social paradigms of disability. On the one hand, they acknowledge a collective commitment to lessen the obstacles to a dignified life. On the other hand, pensions for veterans clearly illustrate the assumptions of the medical model, from disability-as-personhood to disability-as-inability to the expectation of occasional "cures."

The first substantive change in the Civil War pension scheme is a case in point. Having two years earlier initiated a schedule of monthly payments based on military rank and on undefined "total" and "inferior" categories of disability, Congress added in 1864 a list of service-related "losses" (of a hand, a foot, eyesight, and so on) that qualified a veteran for specified payments. The Pension Bureau eventually extended the schedule of conditions to include payments for loss of fingers (with varying amounts for index and other fingers) and toes (distinguishing between big and other toes). These legislative and bureaucratic efforts to construct a hierarchy of abnormalities acknowledged the symbolic logic of the medical model – the missing body part or function *was* the diminished veteran, and a standard monthly payment was the appropriate response once the condition (and its service origin) had been identified.[16]

Other tenets of the medical model had long influenced veterans' pensions. As it developed a system of benefits for veterans of the Revolutionary War, Congress began to require applicants to demonstrate that a war-related disability prevented them from "obtaining [their] livelihood, by labor." Lawmakers returned to this equation of disability and inability after the Civil War. In 1866, while expanding the specific "losses" eligible for pensions, they created a new category of payments for veterans who depended on "constant personal aid and attention," another for those who were "incapacitated for performing any manual labor," and a third for those whose disability equaled the loss of a limb. In 1890, Congress further affirmed the functionality principle by creating a new type of pension that ignored a disability's origin and was entirely based on inability "to earn a support."[17]

Pension legislation also had a long-standing link to the expectation that some disabilities could be "cured." Revolutionary War pensions had required recipients to submit to biennial examinations by a physician to verify the disability's persistence. The rule was reinstated before the Civil War and continued into the 1870s, when a pension commissioner pointed out that "there will be very few cases in which the disability of so long standing, in men of such advanced years as have now been reached by the survivors of the late war, will become of less degree than it now is." Congress accordingly dropped the re-examination requirement, but the commissioner's statement acknowledged the persistence of the rehabilitation assumption.[18]

Throughout their nineteenth-century changes, Civil War pension laws remained connected to the principle of self-government. Current self-sufficiency, a key component of self-government, disqualified a veteran from a pension unless he had a specific "loss"; given prevailing doubts about "inferior" races' ability to govern themselves, this policy would seem to be biased against those whose traits were most to be admired.

But pension policy also required evidence of *past* self-government. Before 1890, pensionable disabilities had to originate in the line of duty; by the 1870s, the Pension Bureau was instructing examining physicians to determine how "the habits of the applicant seem to affect his disability," a requirement that was enacted into law as a proscription of "vicious habits" in 1890. Both policies allowed officials to examine veterans' prior behavior for devotion to duty and self-control.[19]

Federal benefits for Civil War veterans thus evolved against a background of assumptions about behavior and character. Self-government drew explicit attention, expressed in pension commissioners' reports as well as in legislation. The ideal beneficiary, according to one commissioner, was the veteran who "freely and promptly, as soon as the occasion [arose]," defended his country "at the peril and if need be at the sacrifice of his life." Wartime moral fortitude presumably continued afterward, and these same patriots "have been modest in preferring claims for pensions."[20]

By the same logic, absence of self-discipline in time of war also persisted in civilian life. Driven by "insatiable greed," the same men who "crowd themselves to the front at soldiers' gatherings [and] clamor for resolutions for more pensions" had been "the bounty jumpers, cowards, and deserters, and the fraudulent malingerers" during the War. If self-discipline at any time meant self-discipline all the time, officials could cast a wide net for signs of pension-worthiness, especially when records of disability origin were unclear or "vicious habits" were at issue.[21]

Race and ethnicity were bound up with fitness for self-government in Gilded-Age thought, but they are harder to locate in pension officials' testimony. African Americans and the foreign-born made up a substantial share of the veteran population: the U.S. Colored Troops were more than 8 percent of the Union army and foreign-born soldiers were an additional 24 percent. We have seen that, authorized by federal law, officials were eager to analyze veterans' character and motivation. The laws gave little encouragement to a discussion of race and ethnicity, however, and with exceptions that will be described in Chapter 3, administrators seldom mentioned these topics.[22]

Yet official pronouncements take us only so far. Pension administrators commented most often on problems that seemed the most intractable, such as pension attorneys' machinations and legislatively imposed flaws in the method of verifying applicants' eligibility. Beliefs about race and ethnicity, on the other hand, are meant to *avoid* intractability by explaining past and predicting future behavior. When a special examiner investigated John Schumacher's pension application in 1890, for example, the judgment that Schumacher was "an ignorant German" was meant to explain why he had not better documented his claim.[23]

Because race and ethnicity were widely assumed to be valid explanations of character and behavior, benefits administrators may have acted on the basis of these concepts without routinely discussing them. If African Americans and immigrants, on the other hand, saw race and ethnicity as less significant than manhood, they would have been especially willing to claim their rights to benefits that recognized patriotic self-sacrifice.

After Chapter 2 explores the political forces that, in addition to Gilded-Age ideologies, shaped the Civil War pension system, subsequent chapters investigate veterans' initiatives and other participants' practices as they shaped the federal government's system of pensions and soldiers' homes.

2

The Moral Economy of Veterans' Benefits

The evolution of the federal government's Civil War pension system presents a conundrum. In an age much better known for Social Darwinism than for social insurance, Congress created a program that benefited as many as 745,000 veterans at a time and ultimately cost more than $5 billion. The program began with the "general law" of 1862, the basic provisions of which prevailed until 1890. As we saw in Chapter 1, this series of laws primarily embodied the "medical" approach to disability. Monthly payments for specified "losses" began in 1864 with $20 for both feet and $25 for both hands or both eyes, and reached a maximum of $100 in 1889 for loss of both hands. Lawmakers also established categories of aid for veterans who relied on caregivers, were unable to do manual labor, or had a disability equivalent to loss of a limb. The general law used local physicians to verify applicants' conditions and to provide fractional ratings for ailments such as rheumatism, liver disease, and sunstroke, as long as they were traceable to military service.[1]

Congress altered the general law's procedures, though not its foundations, in 1879. Approved pensions had been funded previously as of the application date, but after a campaign of lobbying led by pension attorneys, lawmakers authorized "arrears" payments covering the time between a soldier's discharge and his pension application. Average annual pension expenses, which had held near $30 million in the 1870s, more than doubled in the 1880s, and pensions became an increasingly potent political issue.[2]

A fundamental change to the pension system occurred in 1890. After failing to override Grover Cleveland's veto of a similar measure three years earlier, Congress obtained Benjamin Harrison's approval of a bill creating the "disability law" pension system. The new law altered two of the general law's approaches to disability: it authorized payments of $6 to $12 a month for nearly any disability a veteran could demonstrate, regardless of when it originated, and it abandoned payments for specific disabilities, calling instead for a pension "rating" based entirely on inability to perform manual labor. This widening of eligibility generated another near-doubling of average annual expenditures to $122 million in the 1890s. Anticipating the "service pension" law (pensions for military service alone) of 1907, the Pension Bureau began in the 1890s to award the minimum payment to applicants over 65 years of age unless they showed "unusual vigor and ability for the performance of manual labor in one of that age," and a presidential order lowered this automatically pensionable age to 62 in 1904.[3]

Taken together, these pension policies' most striking feature is their steadily rising inclusiveness. Policy makers' extension of coverage to more and more veterans is especially impressive in view of the Gilded Age's hostility to social programs in general and the bitter condemnations of pension expansion in particular. Critics denounced the disability law of 1890 as "socialism of an extreme and dangerous type" because it opened the door to "the pollution of the pension roll" by men who were "idle, given to rum, and lazy." How could so expansive a social program flourish in an era so inhospitable toward aid to individuals?[4]

Previous explorations of this question have produced two plausible answers. First, precedents existed for progressively liberalized aid to American veterans. Drawing on principles that stretched back through colonial times to Elizabethan England, lawmakers experimented with various pension schemes for veterans of the Revolutionary War before establishing a formalized system in 1792. At one time or another, this system included the hallmarks (occupational definition of disability, physician investigation of claims, and so on) that would later characterize Civil War pensions; Congress also adopted major expansions of coverage in 1818 and 1832, the latter change resulting in a service pension. Veterans of the War of 1812, the Mexican War, and pre–Civil War

Indian conflicts were likewise granted initial pensions for disability, and eventually were made eligible for service pensions.[5]

Lawmakers who debated Civil War pensions were well aware of these precedents. As the Senate considered service-pension legislation in 1907, for example, one member argued that "both in reference to the time elapsing after the close of the War and the length of service necessary to entitle a soldier to the benefits of the law, and in reference to the amount received, the soldiers of previous wars have in some respects been treated with greater consideration than those of the Civil War."[6]

A second explanation for the growth of Civil War pensions is their rise to prominence in Gilded-Age politics. In the wake of the arrears law, partisan politics and constituency service created three increasingly potent driving forces behind pension generosity. First, although both parties sought advantage from arrears legislation, Republican leaders and officials of the Grand Army of the Republic, the largest Civil War veterans' group, joined with pension attorneys in mobilizing ex-soldiers on behalf of Republicans who pledged to further extend pension benefits. This potent campaign culminated in the vetoed disability pension bill of 1887 and the approved pension act of 1890.[7]

Second, members of Congress took two kinds of direct interest in the awarding of pensions. When legislative changes such as the arrears and disability laws triggered a flood of new applications, the accumulating cases created a backlog of hundreds of thousands of applications and long delays in processing the claims. Impatient veterans and their dependents contacted their member of Congress, who in turn queried the Pension Bureau about the cases in question. A recent study of congressional interventions indicates that they produced results – the odds of approval by the Pension Bureau increased when a lawmaker intervened on behalf of an applicant.[8]

Another form of congressional intervention occurred when applicants were rejected or received an unsatisfactory amount in an approved pension. Some of these dissatisfied pension seekers appealed to their senator or representative, who typically introduced special bills for the aggrieved constituents. The House and Senate, taking pro forma action on sparsely attended "pension days," churned out large numbers of individual pensions: by 1907, lawmakers had passed more than 19,000 of these private pension acts.[9]

Third, with or without congressional intervention, the Pension Bureau occasionally cooperated in partisan maneuvering over pensions. Figure 2–1 shows the yearly approval rate for applications acted upon by the Pension Bureau. Officials blamed dwindling evidence of wartime trauma for the long decline in approvals in the 1870s, and the steady rise at the beginning of the twentieth century is attributable to the adoption of age as a pension qualifier; the other sharp swings in approval rates, however, brought forth charges of partisan manipulation.

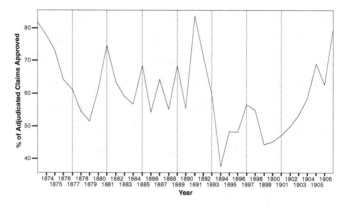

Figure 2-1 Percent of adjudicated pension claims approved, 1873–1907.

Source: Reports of Commissioner of Pensions.

Note: Reference lines indicate changes of presidential administrations.

A former Pension Bureau employee insisted that "just previous to the election [of 1880, the commissioner] concentrated all the available force of his office on Ohio and Indiana pension cases with a view of allowing as many of them as he possibly could, so as to influence the election in those States." When Grover Cleveland gained control of the Pension Bureau after the next election, his commissioner complained that the Bureau had become "all but avowedly a political machine," which "had for the claimant other tests than those of the law." Democrats' pension-approval rates remained fairly high, however, and there is evidence that they also favored "swing" states.[10]

The election of Benjamin Harrison in 1888 ushered in a new era of pension maneuvering. Harrison's first pension

The Pension Building in Washington, D.C., completed in 1887, was modeled on Michelangelo's Palazzo Farnese in Rome. (*Report of Commissioner* [1900])

commissioner, a longtime advocate of pension generosity, announced that "I have the support of the President and the Cabinet on this line – a pension for every old soldier who needs one," and his successor allegedly ordered the Bureau to approve one thousand pensions a day. The resulting surge in pension awards was labeled an "industry of corruption," serving politicians who transformed the Pension Bureau into "the central office through which they have attempted to call up 'the soldier vote.'"[11]

Figure 2–1 indicates that when Cleveland regained power in 1893, his effort to purge the pension rolls of unwarranted beneficiaries, hailed by some as "pension reform" and condemned by others as an "orgy of punishing and humiliating the pensioners of the Civil War," also applied to applications for new and increased pensions. The precipitous drop in pension approvals ended a period in which commissioners actively joined with leaders of both parties to seek the gratitude of individual and organized beneficiaries of the pension system. Analyses of applicants' success presented in Chapters 3 and 4 take account of periods of extraordinary expansion and contraction in pension approvals.[12]

Historical precedent and the ebb and flow of electoral politics thus explain much of the expansion of Civil War pensions, but they leave unanswered a question posed by an early scholar of military benefits. William H. Glasson admitted the potency of precedents and political maneuvering in producing "the most lavish military pension system in the history of the world," yet these forces did not, in his view, render the outcome inevitable. Precedent and politics notwithstanding, Glasson wondered why "the people of the United States have borne the financial burdens of the [pension] system with only a moderate amount of complaint, if not with general contentment." Weighing possibilities such as self-interest and the invisible burden of the tariffs that supported the pension system, Glasson ultimately found no satisfactory reason why criticism of pension expansion was marginalized. A comparison to an earlier paradox in American politics may help with this conundrum and with the issue of discrimination in an inclusive policy.[13]

Recent close reading of revolutionary-era political thought has illuminated the well-known irony presented by demands for liberty by a revolutionary generation that condoned slavery. Leaders of the American Revolution especially prized individual agency – just as one individual could strive for liberty, another could accept servitude. Rebellion, running away, and other forms of resistance represented rejection of slavery, a course of action presumably available to any slave. Race, in this view, was a correlate of slavery, not its determinant. African Americans seemed less likely to reject slavery, but they *could* do so, which would earn them liberty (or punishment) in the same way as breaking with England would earn liberty or punishment for the revolutionaries.[14]

Liberty in this context closely resembles self-government as discussed in Chapter 1. Why then, if people of color could potentially earn liberty, were non-white immigrants not given a chance in the 1790 naturalization law to earn citizenship? A possible reason for the contradictory treatment is that not all circumstances presented equal hazards. Rebellious slaves and insurgent colonists both risked death for their actions; immigration, though it included hardships of its own, did not carry with it the risk of execution. Policy makers thus turned to race, rather than evidence of past behavior, as the predictor of newcomers' "fitness" for self-government. Eligibility for pensions following the Civil War may be viewed in a similar light. The War had provided a universally acknowledged trial in which participants could demonstrate their fitness for government assistance. Anyone, African American or white, native-born or immigrant, could choose to risk this trial. The enabling legislation for pensions made some allowance for African Americans' circumstances: rules for proving marriage, for example, were relaxed for black soldiers' widows and children when they sought pensions. But like the right to liberty, the right to a pension was not irrevocable. The proscription of "vicious habits" that administrators and lawmakers introduced into the pension system was meant to root out those men who "went in for the bounties, with the fighting and the cause of the Union as mere incidents."[15]

Local examining physicians were assigned to investigate pension-seekers' claims for inclusion in the program. By the 1880s, the Pension Bureau had largely replaced its initial complement of individual surgeons with three-member panels, paid by the examination and charged with conducting "thorough and searching" evaluations of each applicant's case. The Bureau refrained from defining "vicious habits" in its instructions; inspection of the certificates filed by examining physicians indicates that they primarily sought evidence of drinking, smoking, and venereal disease. In practice, the physicians rarely mentioned applicants' habits, leaving the claimants to furnish testimonials to their behavior.[16]

The physicians' "rating" of disability was not definitive, however. The Pension Bureau employed legal and medical reviewers who made the final evaluation of pension-seekers' applications, including witnesses' statements, physicians' ratings, and findings of special examiners assigned to especially difficult cases, and who produced a final decision on the amount, if any, each applicant would receive.

Throughout the twists and turns of partisan competition and changes in laws, the Pension Bureau maintained an avowed goal of "justice, and justice alone." To the pension commissioners' chagrin, however, a host of actors seemed to make justice elusive. Pension attorneys and their claim houses, according to commissioners, perverted the approval process, "using perjury, forgery, bribery, and every species of available fraud"; local examining physicians were "assigned to duty without any knowledge of the law, and practically without any experience or instruction," and were "likely to be prejudiced in the favor of claimants"; and the Bureau was deluged with "thousands of letters ... each week from claimants, from attorneys, from members of Congress, and other persons urging immediate action in certain pension cases," when such contacts "serve only to retard the work and fritter away the time of the clerical force."[17]

Much of this frustration came from cognitive dissonance between the officials' professed devotion to justice and the actual standard by which the Bureau was judged – in the words of a former employee, each commissioner sought to show "that he has transacted a larger volume of business than his predecessor." In pursuit of this goal, commissioners occasionally ordered a speedup, epitomized by the peak year of 1891–92, when the Bureau approved more

The Pension Building's equally impressive Great Hall was designed after Michelangelo's Church of Santa Maria degli Angeli. (*Report of Commissioner* [1900])

than 311,000 applications. Because the Bureau employed only forty-seven medical reviewers and referees to pass final judgment on disability claims in that year, such campaigns helped to inspire headlines such as "Pension Office Stupidity," and to confirm historians' judgment of the Bureau's ineptitude.[18]

Yet the Pension Bureau was by no means unique. Other divisions in the Interior Department experienced worse mismanagement, and the agencies charged with administering the Chinese exclusion laws were also plagued by corruption, fraud, and public criticism. A recent study of immigration enforcement, however, argues that administration should not be judged solely on the number of frauds detected and prospective entrants turned away. Instead of frustration over the worsening record on these measures of performance, the system's managers expressed satisfaction with their procedures because, having received complete authority over the admission process, the Bureau of Immigration crafted the process into a meaningful ritual: each routine examination affirmed the power of the United States over would-be immigrants and reassured administrators that their standardized procedures had imposed order and rationality on a heretofore intractable problem. Should we reinterpret the Pension Bureau's practices in the same way?[19]

A stark difference between the Bureau of Immigration and the Pension Bureau is that the latter never received the consolidated authority it requested. Pension commissioners ceaselessly complained that they lacked the power to challenge the testimony that applicants submitted to substantiate their claims. One commissioner devised a solution, which would divide the nation into sixty districts and would assign a government-employed physician and a clerk to each district, eliminating the local boards of contract physicians (as well as the need for special examiners to follow up on difficult or suspicious claims). The physician would conduct all medical examinations and the clerk would interrogate witnesses, making a Bureau-controlled face-to-face encounter the key to the approval process. The Senate approved this proposal in 1881, but it died in the House, apparently through the lobbying efforts of the largest claim house.[20]

Deprived of the "direct, unmediated encounter between government official and applicant" that was the centerpiece of immigration enforcement, the Pension Bureau was left with medical encounters it did not trust and statements by applicants' friends and neighbors it could not question. As applications piled up and the clamor for production of pension certificates became more intense, it would be surprising not to find Bureau reviewers falling back on simple formulations of race and ethnicity to judge the validity of claims from men who had served in the U.S. Colored Troops or had foreign-sounding names.[21]

Race and ethnicity may also have affected the pension system in more indirect ways. Applying for a pension was a complex process: a pension-seeker began by describing his military service and disability to the Pension Bureau, which sought confirmation from the War Department and often asked applicants (or special examiners) to obtain corroboration from comrades, commanders, neighbors, and other witnesses. When his application was thus far acceptable, the veteran was instructed to report for a medical examination. After the physicians made their recommendations and the Bureau's reviewers made their decisions, rejected applicants could appeal the ruling or file a new claim if new disabilities arose; pensioners could also request payment increases when the law changed.[22]

Calling for know-how and willingness to navigate bureaucratic intricacies, this process could discourage veterans with limited English skills, those whose service records were hard to locate due to a changed slave name or a variously spelled foreign name, and those unable to travel for medical examinations. On the other hand, in exchange for a government-regulated fee, claim houses offered to help veterans with their applications. Nevertheless, studies of pension applicants have found a substantially lower proportion of applications among black veterans, and this book explores more deeply the causes and consequences of African Americans' and immigrants' willingness to seek a pension.[23]

An additional question that underlies this study is the extent to which race and ethnicity affected production of a meaning for "disability." Under the general law, the leading basis of pension claims was gunshot wounds, but the next most common condition among pensioners was diarrhea. Devising a meaning for disability was a contributory process, originating in the conditions that veterans described in their applications, undergoing modification by examining physicians, and culminating in judgment by the Pension Bureau.[24]

This was also, as we have seen, a contentious process, caught up in the strain between the Bureau and examining physicians. Indeed, the nature of the two parties' mutual distrust points to differences that were deep enough to affect the definition of disability. The Bureau and its examining physicians disagreed about the use of evidence: Bureau officials' insistence that physicians' ratings were inaccurate and inconsistent implied misinterpretation of evidence, and physicians felt that the Bureau's procedures withheld vital evidence from the examination. Asked about the value of applicants' medical histories in conducting proper examinations, one physician could not mask his resentment: "Just what evidence ... is required by the Pension Office in cases of disability, my position does not require me to know. ... As I understand, the Pension Office does require affidavits from physicians and friends and neighbors of the applicant, but the precise nature and character of the evidence so required it is not within my province to know."[25]

Administrators in Washington and local examining boards thus had separate ways of investigating disability, beginning with the evidence presented by applicants. The next four chapters investigate the influence of race and ethnicity on the disabilities that applicants presented, how physicians and administrators participated in generating meaning, how claim houses participated in the process, and how veterans decided to obtain institutional care.

This study seeks to answer the fundamental questions outlined in this chapter, but in the nature of such investigations, questions inevitably beget other questions. The study's focus is primarily on individuals, but it would be short-sighted to overlook the development of the organizations charged with administering veterans' benefits. Subsequent chapters use the issues of race and ethnicity to examine the functioning of pension administration and the evolution of federal homes for veterans with disabilities.

3

African-American Veterans and the Pension System

Pension officials conducted no extensive discussion of race, but they did say enough to reveal solicitude mixed with suspicion of black veterans and their survivors. Investigators showed sympathy for Southern black pensioners who were intimidated or tricked into paying extortionate fees to claim houses, and the Pension Bureau helped special examiners to ascertain dates for ex-slaves and to retrace survivors' migrations. On the other hand, the same guidelines warned examiners that African-American

Some of this material appeared earlier in *The Journal of Interdisciplinary History*, XXXVIII (2008), 377–399. It is included herein with the permission of the editors of The Journal of Interdisciplinary History and The MIT Press, Cambridge, Massachusetts. © 2008 by the Massachusetts Institute of Technology and The Journal of Interdisciplinary History, Inc.

widows might claim benefits for children not belonging to their husband, and officials were prone to posit racial explanations for applicants' behavior: a special examiner declared that "those of that race who can be counted reliable and absolutely truthful, are a rarity indeed," and a government auditor wondered at "the general credulity with which the race is apt to listen to the proposals of a *sharper*."[1]

To understand the role of race in the Civil War pension system, these glimpses of official attitudes must be supplemented with the experiences of veterans such as Clay Ballard. Born a slave in Kentucky, Ballard enlisted in the 116th Colored Infantry in 1864, survived the War without serious disease or injury, and was discharged in 1867. Ballard returned to Kentucky, where he and his wife ran a boardinghouse until his health declined in the late 1880s. After Congress enacted the disability law in 1890, Ballard submitted his first pension application, citing rheumatism and scurvy. Despite the testimony of a private physician that Ballard was "unfit for hard manual labor," his examining surgeons found no pensionable disabilities. Ballard asked that a reevaluation be conducted in Cincinnati, insisting that "I did not receive a fair and impartial examination" because no "colored ex-soldier can get justice from that board [in Lexington, Kentucky]." Ballard received another examination (in Frankfort, Kentucky) and the physicians found him partially disabled, but this time the Pension Bureau's reviewers rejected the claim. Ballard filed a new application claiming additional disabilities in 1894, but he died the next year before another examination could be scheduled.[2]

Ballard's case would ordinarily have ended at this point, but his widow Mary, assisted by the pension attorney who had represented her husband, pursued his claim in order to obtain a widow's pension. The Pension Bureau stood its ground, insisting in 1897 that Clay Ballard had not been prevented from "earning a support," whereupon the attorney appealed, arguing that "it certainly looks strange ... when soldiers die without being disabled." The Bureau, suspecting that its rejections "cannot now be defended," reopened the case, and after taking depositions, a special examiner decided that Ballard had indeed been "practically totally disabled," clearing the way for Mary Ballard's pension.[3]

Other than Clay Ballard's initial complaint and an endorsement as "one of the better class of negroes," race is largely absent from his pension file. It would be premature, however, to conclude that Ballard was the victim of a simple oversight. Did other African Americans disproportionately share Ballard's acknowledged mistreatment at the hands of the Pension Bureau? This chapter seeks an answer to this question, beginning with racial differences in service-related disabilities and continuing through black veterans' willingness to seek pensions and their experience when they did apply.[4]

Stark differences in the Civil War–era experiences of white and African-American soldiers shaped the profile of

[Date of Examination.]

We hereby certify that in compliance with the requirements of the law we have carefully examined this applicant, who states that he is suffering from the following disability, incurred in the service, viz: *Rheumatism. Scurvy*

(Acts June 27/90

and that he receives a pension of _____ dollars per month.

He makes the following statement upon which he bases his claim for *original.*

[Original, increase, restoration, &c.]

Contracted Rheumatism and scurvy during the war. Was costive. Has pains in arms & legs. Had a chancre & non-suppurating bubo in New Orleans, during the war. Has young heart some years ago. No other allegation

Upon examination we find the following objective conditions: Pulse rate, __80__; respiration, __18__; temperature, __98__; height, __5__ feet __7__ inches; weight, __200__ pounds; age, __50__ years.

Claimant is fat and well nourished. His heart is nor-
~~mal in all respects. Joints, muscles, tendons and fibrous~~
structures are all normal. No evidence of any rheumatism.
He has not a tooth in his head. Claimant has a phymosis
~~probably due to the chancre that he had in New Orleans during~~
the war. No evidence of any Syphilis. He is very bald headed. No other diability found to exist.

_____ He is, in our opinion, entitled to a _____
rating for the disability caused by _____, _____ for that caused by _____, and _____ for that caused by _____

_____ Pres. _____, Sec'y. _____, Treas.

GENERAL AFFIDAVIT.

State of _Kentucky_

County of _Fayette_

In the matter of, Claim by _Clay Ballard_
Co. G. 116 Regt- a. S. C. J.

Personally came before me, a NOTARY PUBLIC, in and for said County and State,

Clay Ballard aged_____ years,

and _____ aged_____ years,

citizens of the Town of _Lexington_ County of _Fayette_

State of _Ky._ well known to me to be reputable and entitled to credit and when duly sworn, declare in relation to aforesaid case, as follows:

That I am claimant -above named that- I was examined for my alleged disabilities at Lexington, Ky. before the board of examing surgeons I did not-receive a fair and impartial examination I do not-believe any colored ex-soldier can get-justice from that-board I request that- my claim under act-of June 27, 1890. be reconsidered and that-an order for my medical examination be issued to me to appear before Board No 1 at-Cincinnati, Ohio. #280 West-6th street-in order that-the full extent -of my disabilities may be determined

Examining physicians' "zero rating" of Clay Ballard's pension request (opposite) and his affidavit (above) alleging that no "colored ex-soldier can get justice from that board." (National Archives)

the veteran population. On the one hand, despite the well-known carnage among black soldiers at the Battle of the Crater and the assault on Battery Wagner, the toll of combat fell comparatively lightly on African-American troops as a whole: sixteen per thousand black soldiers were killed in action or died from wounds, less than half of white soldiers' mortality. This difference is attributable partly to black soldiers' shortened time at risk – African Americans did not enter the army in force until the War's third year – and partly to prejudiced commanders, many of whom distrusted African Americans as fighting men and disproportionately assigned them to menial chores.[5]

On the other hand, the ravages of illness more than made up for black soldiers' lessened risk of dying in combat: disease killed 141 per thousand African-American soldiers, versus 59 per thousand white troops. Historians have cited inferior medical care and service in the disease-ridden lower Mississippi Valley to account for black soldiers' greater vulnerability to maladies such as pneumonia, dysentery, and malaria.[6]

Mortality in the army has gained researchers' attention, but we are concerned here with a somewhat different question: were there also racial differences in battle wounds and disease among men who survived the War? Particularly under the general law governing pension eligibility until 1890, existence or absence of a recorded debility could encourage or discourage pension seeking.

Table 3–1 investigates this question by reporting the prevalence of wounds and diseases among two large samples of soldiers who survived the Civil War. This and all subsequent tables are based on random samples of infantry companies collected by Robert W. Fogel and fellow researchers

Table 3-1 *Survivors of the Civil War who had been hospitalized for a wound or illness during service, CPE sample members*

	Whites	African Americans
% hospitalized for wounds	29.0	12.3
% hospitalized for illness	67.7	54.5
Number of cases	26,071	3,852

of the Center for Population Economics at the University of Chicago (see Appendix for a fuller discussion of these data, which are referred to as the CPE samples).

The table's top row reports veterans who had survived at least one battle wound, while the second row tabulates survivors who had been confined to a military hospital with one or more diseases. The first row corresponds to statistics on battle deaths: the proportion of white survivors with battle wounds is more than twice the African-American proportion. The second row, however, appears to contradict the reported prevalence of disease among black troops, because proportionally fewer African-American survivors had suffered from a disease while in the army. A key reason for the discrepancy is the wartime disease toll itself: taking the perspective of soldiers who contracted a disease during their service, 34 percent of black disease sufferers died while still in the army versus 17 percent of white soldiers, leaving proportionally fewer African-American survivors of illness. Black veterans more often returned home without the conditions that would qualify them for a general-law pension, and we would thus expect fewer applications from them at least until 1890.[7]

Slightly fewer than one-third (31.9 percent) of all black enlisted men in the CPE samples ever applied for a pension, whereas more than half (52.5 percent) of white veterans applied. These aggregates, however, mask complexities in gaining access to the pension system: proportionately more white soldiers survived the War (because of white soldiers' lower disease mortality, 85 percent survived versus 79 percent of black recruits), and we cannot assume that any racial difference in application rates remained uniform through changes in pension law.[8]

Table 3–2 allows for these two influences on pension applications. Examining survivors of the War, the table shows the percentage of veterans who applied for a new pension in the first two major periods of pension law (the third period, begun by the service-pension law of 1907, marks the end of this study). The table reveals strikingly different patterns in veterans' behaviors. First, white and African-American veterans reacted differently to the general law – 44 percent of white veterans sought a pension before mid-1890, but fewer than 20 percent of black veterans applied. Under the disability law, however, veterans of both races overwhelmingly sought access to the pension system; indeed, the proportion of African-American veterans who applied exceeded that of whites. This new participation throws the general-law results into sharp relief: why did black veterans disproportionately shy away from the first pension system?[9]

Table 3-2 *Percent of Civil War survivors who applied for a new pension, CPE samples*

	Whites	African Americans
1862–1890	43.9	19.7
1890–1907	91.6	93.6
Number of cases	25,812	3,715

We have already noted the disproportionate absence of wounds and service-related diseases that could have deterred African Americans from seeking a general-law pension, but other explanations must also be considered. Donald R. Shaffer, in his pioneering study of African-American veterans, attributes much of the racial difference in pension-seeking to the disadvantages that black veterans faced in navigating the application process. Because most African-American soldiers had been slaves, and because many ex-slaves were impoverished and illiterate, Shaffer argues that black veterans were especially unlikely to hear about pensions and unable to document their disabilities.[10]

The effects of deprivation under slavery cannot be directly assessed from the CPE data. Because literacy was not recorded for Civil War recruits, applicants' signatures (or marks) on pension records are the principal indicator of sample members' literacy; those who never applied are a mystery. Exploring this influence on pension seeking thus requires information collected during the War, one item of which was soldiers' place of birth.

Birthplace is an excellent proxy for gauging postwar African-American deprivation. Although former servitude is not listed in military records, ex-slaves can reliably be identified from their state and county of birth. In the 1860 census, 99.6 percent of the black population in thirteen Southern states, plus the majority-slave counties of Maryland, were slaves, whereas 93.9 percent of African Americans living elsewhere were free. This slave-versus-free distinction continued to influence literacy and wealth after the Civil War. In 1870, 64 percent of black men aged thirty to fifty who had been born in free states could write, versus 13 percent of those born in slave states; freeborn black men held an average of $436 in property versus $116 for ex-slaves.[11]

Table 3–3 weighs the effect of this distinction against characteristics that were directly related to eligibility for general-law pensions, plus a variable to control for changes in behavior caused by the arrears law of 1879. The table reports the average and a "hazard ratio" for each variable. The latter statistic estimates the effect of each characteristic, with the others held constant, on the probability of applying at a given point in time, compared to an index value of one (see Appendix). Having been hospitalized for a wound, for example, doubled the likelihood of applying compared to a veteran who survived without being wounded. Hazard ratios in boldface meet the conventional .05 test for statistical significance.[12]

Part A of the table shows that having a hospital record inspired pension seeking among both races, but former

Table 3–3 *Comparative influences on the likelihood of applying for a new pension before mid-1890 by race, CPE samples*

A. *Whites and African Americans*

	Whites		African Americans	
Variable	*Mean*	*Hazard Ratio*	*Mean*	*Hazard Ratio*
Hospitalized for wound	.286	**2.19**	.123	**2.21**
Hospitalized for illness	.676	**2.00**	.547	**1.48**
Former slave			.828	**.80**
Control for 1879–80	.187	**3.25**	.119	**5.49**
Number of cases		25,812		3,714

B. *Former Slaves Only*

Variable	*Mean*	*Hazard Ratio*
Hospitalized for wound	.122	**1.97**
Hospitalized for illness	.564	**1.33**
Proportion of company freeborn	.122	1.06
Enlisted in DE/MD/VA/DC	.187	**1.42**
Control for 1879–80	.113	**4.45**
Number of cases		2,761

Note: Hazard ratios in boldface indicate $p < .05$

slaves were nonetheless underrepresented among applicants: wartime health notwithstanding, freedmen were less likely to apply for a general-law pension than were freeborn black veterans. Part B explores this difference by drawing on a study of the CPE samples in which the researchers suggest that interaction between former slaves and free blacks in the army may have contributed to higher literacy among the ex-slaves. It is conceivable that such interaction also instilled the assertiveness needed to apply for pensions, so Part B of Table 3–3 focuses on ex-slaves alone. A variable is added for the percentage of company comrades who were freemen (using the slave-versus-free classification described above), and an additional dummy variable identifies recruits who enlisted in Eastern border areas, which produced the companies with the most freeborn African Americans; the latter variable is meant to estimate interaction between slaves and free blacks *before* the War.[13]

The hazard ratios in Part B indicate that any influence of freeborn comrades on ex-slaves' tendency to seek a general-law pension was overshadowed by the much stronger impact of enlisting (and probably having lived in) a border state, which raised the likelihood of applying by 42 percent. This finding offers some support to the argument that slavery's deprivations discouraged pension seeking: ex-slaves who had grown up in the vicinity of free blacks were more assertive in seeking general-law pensions than were freedmen who had been deprived of this contact.[14]

At the same time, both parts of Table 3–3 show that all black veterans joined their white peers in calculating the chances for a pension. Having a wound, the surest sign of military service's toll on the body, or possessing a record of a service-related illness, sharply raised veterans' propensity to seek a pension. Part of black veterans' reluctance to seek general-law pensions shown in Table 3–2 undoubtedly came from lack of experience and resources for negotiating a bureaucratic maze, but another part was also due to their disproportionate lack of the evidence of wartime trauma.

Table 3–3 cannot capture an additional difference within and between the races. We know little about the health problems of those who did not seek pensions, but death rates suggest that African-American veterans, especially former slaves, disproportionately suffered from poor health. The crude death rate from 1865 to 1890 for members of the CPE samples with known death dates was 15 per thousand person-years for ex-slaves, 10.7 for freeborn black veterans, and 5.6 for whites. The morbidity that undoubtedly underlay this mortality difference may have influenced pension seeking. Though Table 3–3 shows that service-related health problems encouraged black veterans to apply for a pension under the general law, Table 3–2 makes it clear that any such encouragement took place far less often than among whites. *Current* illnesses and injuries, which undoubtedly plagued black veterans more than their white peers, could easily overwhelm health problems that had arisen in the army; if a veteran had been hospitalized for diarrhea and then developed tuberculosis or heart disease after the War, the general law offered him no assistance for these new conditions. As their health continued to worsen, black veterans who survived into the 1890s would have been especially enthusiastic about pensions for recently developed health problems.[15]

Multivariate analysis of pension seeking under the disability law is unnecessary, because the nearly universal participation shown in Table 3–2 leaves little variation to explain. Application procedures under the new law became only slightly easier – military service still had to be proven, and a disability not due to "vicious habits" had to be verified, though the burden of connecting it to the War was lifted. Yet, despite the still-cumbersome bureaucratic rules, former slaves now pursued pensions as eagerly as did white veterans.

The new law's acceptance of current disabilities was potentially enough to trigger a flood of new applications, but if ex-slaves were to participate, they would have to learn about the law's provisions and decide to confront the pension system's intricacies. Contemporary developments, including a campaign in the 1890s aimed at persuading Congress to create a system of bonuses and pensions for all former slaves, undoubtedly encouraged ex-slaves to apply for military pensions. The ex-slave plan was never enacted, but pension officials were sufficiently worried about confusion between existing and proposed pensions to order repeated investigations into the ex-slave plan's promoters. The promoters were "setting the negroes wild," wrote one investigator, "robbing them of their money and making anarchists of them." As an ex-slave pension association formed new chapters and pension advocacy spread by word of mouth, black veterans were undoubtedly emboldened to apply for conventional Civil War pensions.[16]

Claim houses and their agents also redoubled their efforts to stimulate new pension applications in the wake of the disability law. A member of Congress declared that claim agents were "writing all over the country, ... hunting up everybody to whom we owe anything," and a Southern pension attorney allegedly announced that "'Pensions for everybody' was henceforth to be the rule of the Pension Bureau"; it was reported that "the colored people responded with great alacrity." The heavy reliance on claim houses, which had already been greater among African-American than white veterans, became nearly universal after 1890.[17]

It is improbable that any single post-1890 change eliminated the racial difference in pension seeking. Once combined, however, the provisions of the new law and the pension-seeking crusades contributed to a revolution in behavior: in an era usually known for proscription and violence directed at African Americans, black veterans asserted their right to participate as equals in a government program.

The case of Willis Pleasant points to the complexity of black veterans' behavior, and raises questions about their treatment in the pension system. Pleasant, like Clay

Ballard, enlisted in a Kentucky regiment of the U.S. Colored Troops, but Pleasant had extensive health problems while in uniform: serving in Kentucky after the end of hostilities, Pleasant sought medical attention on fourteen occasions for maladies including diarrhea, rheumatism, and a foot injury. Pleasant submitted his first pension application in 1890, and his actions suggest that he had just discovered the system. He first applied under the disability law, then supplemented the claim with another in 1891, citing the military origins of his present neuralgia and intestinal disorder. Examining surgeons rated Pleasant as one-third disabled under the disability law, but the Pension Bureau rejected the recommendation, and both surgeons and the Bureau rejected Pleasant's general-law claim. In 1900, because Pleasant was well past the recently defined age of "senility," he was granted a pension of $8 a month. Were white applicants treated in the same manner as was Pleasant? How much did his race, and that of other applicants, influence pension-approval decisions?[18]

To explore this question, we shift the focus from the actions of veterans to the applications they submitted and the way in which they were judged. Pension-Bureau reviewers' rejection of physicians' findings for both Clay Ballard and Willis Pleasant underscores the uneasy relationship between the two groups of evaluators and reminds us that we must examine both stages of decision making.

Table 3–4 shows the results of these decisions. Judgments by both physicians and the Pension Bureau are presented

Table 3–4 *Examining physicians' pension recommendations and Pension Bureau awards by race, applicants for new pensions in CPE samples*

A. Physicians' Recommendations

	1862–1890	1890–1907
% of white applicants recommended for a pension	75.1	90.4
% of African-American applicants recommended for a pension	67.2	78.5
Number of examinations	8,176	6,342

B. Pension Bureau Awards

% of white applicants awarded a pension	77.9	72.5
% of African-American applicants awarded a pension	39.5	45.7
Number of rulings	7,993	6,160

as dichotomies: additional gradations of "success" were possible because applicants could be awarded varying payments under the law, but the starkest difference, and the one most likely to elicit the resentment expressed by Clay Ballard, was the distinction between a pension and no pension. The decision to admit an applicant to the pension system was likewise more significant than were judgments on subsequent payment increases, so the analysis focuses on the results of first pension applications.[19]

The table reveals racial differences at each stage of evaluation. Examining physicians recommended most applicants for a pension, but were more likely to reject African Americans than whites. And there was a much larger disparity in the Pension Bureau's final awards – medical reviewers approved barely half as many African American as white applicants per hundred under the general law, and fewer than two-thirds as many after 1890.

Each of these disparities raises suspicion of prejudice, and the very different circumstances of the evaluations call for separate analyses of decision making. Required by the Pension Bureau to provide a "full symptom-picture of each case," the local contract surgeons were necessarily interested in bodies. The physicians occasionally noted an applicant's "complexion" in their official report, but even if they did not, the color of applicants' skin was inescapable in a face-to-face encounter. Information on sample members' skin color is also available in the CPE data, recorded at the time of enlistment. Two-thirds of sample members from the U.S. Colored Troops were described as "black" or "dark," with other adjectives, especially "light," "yellow," and "mulatto," applied to lighter-skinned recruits. If racism did sway examining physicians' behavior, it should show itself especially clearly among darker-skinned applicants.[20]

Table 3–5 analyzes the results of these examinations for first-time pension seekers. The analysis includes African Americans' skin color and other variables, such as military rank, location of the examination, characteristics of the application, and political timing, that might have influenced the physicians' recommendations. Application characteristics

Table 3–5 *Comparative odds of a favorable pension recommendation by examining physicians, first-time white and African-American applicants in CPE samples*

Variable	1862–1890		1890–1907	
	Mean	*Odds Ratio*	*Mean*	*Odds Ratio*
Applicant's age	51.1	**1.009**	56.5	1.004
Noncommissioned officer	.075	1.120	.067	.939
Examined in 1880	.037	.955		
Examined in second half of Harrison's term			.746	**1.304**
Examined in Cleveland's second term			.080	**.194**
Examined in South	.112	.858	.161	**.775**
Number of disabilities claimed	2.18	**1.116**	3.50	**1.104**
Claims included mental illness	.034	**.693**	.061	**.672**
Applicant described wartime disability origin	.374	**1.384**		
Applicant asserted inability for manual labor			.079	**1.404**
Light-skinned African American	.007	.894	.018	**.601**
Dark-skinned African American	.032	**.635**	.073	**.451**
Weighted number of applicants		8,468		6,369

Note: Odds ratios in boldface indicate $p < .05$

include the number of disabilities each applicant claimed, whether he explicitly tied his condition to current law by referring to its wartime origin or its effect on manual labor, and whether his claims bore the "stigma" of mental illness. The latter was the nineteenth century's preeminent disease of culpability: if wounds and amputations were the visible signs of self-sacrifice, "nervous debility" and related complaints were typically interpreted as signs of defective willpower. Though some late-nineteenth-century clinicians were coming to accept mental illness as a legitimate disease, it remained suspect enough to serve as the benchmark for official distrust of disease claims.[21]

Table 3–5 reports an average value for each variable, plus an "odds ratio," the interpretation of which resembles that of the hazard ratio in Table 3–4: the statistic shows the effect of each characteristic on the odds of receiving a favorable rating, with the other variables held constant (see Appendix). These ratios point to substantial changes in examining physicians' behavior across the two pension eras. Under the general law, examining boards were to identify current disabilities and judge whether they originated in the line of duty. In doing so, the physicians paid little attention to applicants' military rank, and took no discernible part in any rash of pension approvals associated with the 1880 election.[22]

Three elements of pension seekers' own description of their disabilities did influence the examining physicians. The number of health problems asserted by applicants

affected the discovery of a pensionable one (each additional claimed disability raised the odds of approval by
nearly 12 percent), and a veteran's insistence that his
disability originated in the service raised the odds of success by nearly 40 percent. On the other hand, if the applicant claimed "nervous debility" or another psychological
condition, he lowered his entire application's chances by
nearly one-third.

What the physicians saw for themselves is reflected in
their response to the applicant's age – each additional year
raised the odds of approval by 1 percent – and to the color
of his skin. The physicians made no appreciable distinction between whites and light-skinned African Americans
under the general law, but examiners were considerably less
likely to recommend a dark-skinned African American for
a pension.

The physicians' behavior changed under the disability
law. They were still swayed by the number of claimed disabilities and by law-specific language describing applicants'
condition, and were still hostile to mental-illness claims, but
physicians now de-emphasized age as a deciding factor even
as they became more open to other influences. Clay Ballard,
for example, was partly justified in his complaint about a
Southern examining board: an appreciable disparity now
developed between examining boards in the South and those
elsewhere, but it applied to applicants of both races. Because
overall approval rates rose in both the North and South,
the regional gap probably had as much to do with politically

inspired generosity in the North as with evaluative rigor in the South.[23]

Examining physicians were also caught up in the surge of pension approvals during the post-disability-law years of Benjamin Harrison's presidency, and they were on the front lines of Grover Cleveland's campaign against alleged pension fraud – all else equal, applicants saw their odds of a favorable finding fall by 80 percent during Cleveland's second administration. The effect of Cleveland's policies is striking, especially in light of the logistical challenge of changing the behavior of more than 4,000 local surgeons. Pension officials could not replace the physicians wholesale, but the Bureau did carry out its reaction against Harrison's practices in other effective ways: officials ordered repeat medical examinations for pensioners whose awards were now in question, and rescinded physicians' authority to recommend specific pension amounts (the latter power was restored by law in 1895). Local physicians, prodded by the implied warning in the re-examination policy, were key participants in Cleveland's rollback of pension generosity, as reflected in the dramatic drop in approvals shown in Table 3–5.[24]

The physicians also stepped up their discrimination against black applicants. Medical judgments should have been simpler under the disability law: when a current disability was identified and the applicant's behavior was ruled out as the cause, physicians had no need for difficult conjecture about the disability's origins. Yet this was the time when examining physicians were open to political influence, and now they used skin color more starkly in their judgments. Under the disability law, a light-skinned African American saw his chances of a favorable rating fall by 40 percent compared to a white applicant's, and a dark-skinned applicant's chances fell by more than 50 percent.[25]

One physician testified that "it is very natural to form an opinion of a man's character when you examine him .... If he appears like an honest man and not disposed to exaggerate, we are very likely to give him the benefit of the doubt." We described in Chapter 1 the rising importance of race in the late nineteenth century, a development that coincided with examining physicians' increasing equation of skin color and honesty. Intensifying racism does not, however, explain physicians' increasing vulnerability to political currents. The physicians' burgeoning workload, on the other hand, accords with both of these trends.[26]

Administrators expanded the number of local examining boards late in the century, but they could not keep pace with the flood of new applications spurred by legislative changes. In 1874–75 approximately 1,500 physicians conducted 24,000 examinations; nine years later the complement of physicians was nearly 2,000, performing 131,000 examinations; in 1891–92 there were 4,000 physicians, but they now performed more than 430,000 examinations (a disparity that was amplified in the later periods by the requirement that most examinations be done by three physicians). Under these conditions, the Pension Bureau's call for thorough examinations constituted wishful thinking.

Although this sheet-music cover appears to be respectful of black veterans, the lyrics, published in 1905, include a time-worn slur in the line "I am just a Yankee Doodle son of Ham." (Courtesy of Sheet Music Collection, John Hay Library, Brown University)

As demands for results intensified, it was easy to substitute Bureau commitments to generosity or rigor for grounded medical judgments, and even easier to fall back on simple formulations that made race a signifier of character.[27]

If they managed to gain the examining physicians' recommendation, black pension seekers still had to receive final approval from the Pension Bureau's reviewers and referees. Table 3–4 shows a much higher racial disparity in Bureau approvals than at the hands of the physicians, a gap that was uninfluenced by skin color. Occasional references to complexion (in service verification provided by the War Department or in other pension documents) made little difference to the Bureau: reviewers approved 46 percent of black applicants identified as "light" in pension documents, and 47 percent of those listed as "dark." Do the apparent explanations for examining physicians' decisions also account for the actions of the Pension Bureau's reviewers?[28]

Table 3–6 investigates the Pension Bureau's evaluation of both pension seekers and the physicians who had examined them. The table focuses on veterans who had already obtained a pension recommendation from a local board of examining surgeons (or, in the early years, from a single examining physician). It also reports averages and odds ratios for variables that could be expected to influence decisions by officials scrutinizing pension files and physicians' reports; the odds ratios estimate the effect of each variable on the likelihood that a physician's recommendation would be *reversed* (i.e., a ratio less than one indicates a tendency

Table 3–6 *Comparative odds of Pension Bureau reversal, first-time white and African-American applicants in CPE samples who had been approved by examining physicians*

Variable	Before 1890		1890–1907	
	Mean	*Odds Ratio*	*Mean*	*Odds Ratio*
Applicant's age	51.3	**1.008**	56.5	**.983**
Noncommissioned officer	.079	**.698**	.065	.971
Military hospital record	.758	**.830**		
Assisted by claim house	.862	**.685**	.893	.990
Examined in 1880	.037	**.476**		
Examined in second half of Harrison's term			.772	**.514**
Examined in Cleveland's second term			.055	1.281
Number of disabilities claimed	2.15	.954	3.56	**.823**
Claims included mental illness	.031	**1.590**	.060	**1.394**
Applicant described wartime disability origin	.386	**1.166**		
Applicant asserted inability for manual labor			.082	.881
African American	.035	**4.141**	.085	**2.282**
Weighted number of applicants	5,680		5,437	

Note: Odds ratios in boldface indicate $p < .05$

to let a recommendation stand, whereas a ratio higher than one points to a characteristic likely to produce a rejection of the physician's findings).[29]

We noted in Chapter 2 that Congress denied the Pension Bureau the complete control that would have made the approval process an administratively satisfying ritual, but this failure could not ultimately deprive the procedure of its meaning. "A rigid compliance with such rules and regulations as are deemed essential," as one commissioner put it, would bring at least a measure of order to the pandemonium over pensions. The value of applicants' compliance is especially clear under the general law: existence of a military hospital record to establish wartime trauma reduced the odds of a Bureau reversal by nearly 20 percent, and despite officials' relentless criticism of pension attorneys and claim houses, the assistance of a claim house in completing forms and obtaining supplementary testimony lowered the likelihood of a reversal by more than 30 percent.[30]

At the same time, the Bureau balanced compliance with credibility. Examining physicians had, in the Bureau's eyes, undervalued the importance of military rank in making a general-law case, and officials gave preference to former corporals and sergeants under the general law. The Bureau also distrusted the physicians' interpretation of age. A medical referee framed the problem in the 1870s: "It is comparatively rare that claim is now made for a disability contracted in service; it is a question of *sequels* to disabilities incurred in service." Table 3–6 suggests that Bureau officials disapproved of physicians' diagnoses of these sequels: where physicians (according to Table 3–5) were more likely to identify a service-related disability in older applicants, the Bureau was prone to *reverse* this judgment. Thomas French, for example, who gave his age as sixty when he applied for a general-law pension in 1886, received a physician rating of total disability for a hernia dating from 1862; the Pension Bureau, however, rejected the claim.[31]

French was caught up in another point of Pension Bureau mistrust, because he referred in his application to the wartime origin of his disability. We have seen in Table 3–5 that these assertions helped to gain the physicians' recommendation, but they had the opposite effect on the Bureau's reviewers. Table 3–6 shows that the Bureau, apparently convinced that examining physicians were overly credulous about applicants' narratives, was more likely to reject an application when it included a statement of wartime causation.

The Bureau was even more suspicious of applicants and physicians when claims included mental illness. Though physicians had already singled out such claims for disapproval, the presence of a mental illness attracted Pension Bureau distrust of the physicians' rigor as well as the applicant's disability, compounding the official disapproval of psychological impairment.

Under the disability law, applicants continued to bolster their cases by using the language of the new legislation to insist on their incapacity for manual labor, and Table 3–5 showed that this assertion raised the odds of a favorable recommendation from examining physicians. Table 3–6 indicates that the Bureau was no longer as skeptical of such tactics as it had been under the general law; indeed, the Bureau now began to relax other aspects of its insistence on compliance and credibility. Reviewers no longer showed a preference for applications with claim-house assistance, they looked favorably on applicants with large numbers of claimed disabilities (except when these included a mental illness), and they dropped their favoritism for noncommissioned officers. Reviewers were also required to favor older applicants as the Bureau adopted age as a pension qualifier.

Political crosscurrents periodically disrupted the Bureau's maintenance of order. The Bureau, rather than examining physicians, produced the rash of approvals before the 1880 election, and Tables 3–5 and 3–6 indicate that both groups generated the approval surge during Harrison's term (physicians were then more likely to recommend a pension than at any other time under the disability law, and the Bureau was only half as likely as usual to reverse the finding). On the other hand, physicians rejected so many applications during Cleveland's second term that the Bureau's reviewers could essentially endorse the physicians' decisions and still achieve a massive reduction in new pensions.

Amid changes in pension officials' vigilance over veterans' benefits, race stood as the most consistently potent means of judging the credibility of both applicants and examining physicians. After the physicians had disproportionately rejected dark-complected applicants under the general law and all African Americans under the disability law, the Bureau demonstrated its distrust of applicants' credibility and physicians' judgment by adding still more race-based rejections: the Bureau was more than four times as likely to overturn a pension recommendation for an African American as for a white applicant under the general law, and more than twice as likely under the disability law. Why did the Pension Bureau so decisively compound the racial discrimination initiated by the examining physicians?

We suggested above that examining physicians' rising workload contributed to their increasing racial bias. Because medical reviewers had to pass final judgment on pension applications, they faced the same caseload with far fewer workers. While there were approximately 2,000 physicians to perform 131,000 examinations in 1883–84, for example, there were twenty-two referees and reviewers to judge the results; the Bureau's medical staff reached a temporary peak in 1891–92, when forty-six reviewers confronted more than 430,000 examination reports. As the Pension Bureau weathered changes in pension policies, administrative agendas, and an increasingly unmanageable caseload, race was surely as appealing a shortcut to judgment for Bureau reviewers as it was for examining physicians.[32]

If these suggested connections between discrimination and the pension caseload have merit, they should appear in the actions of pension evaluators as their caseload increased. Table 3–7 follows applications through the review process

Table 3-7 *Race, pension rejections, and the application caseload*

Period (Annual Caseload)	*Rejections per 100 New Applications**	
	White Applicants in CPE Samples	*African-American Applicants in CPE Samples*
1862–1880 (under 50,000)	35	26
1881–1882 (50,000–100,000)	42	66
1883–1889 (100,000–200,000)	35	64
1890–1907 (200,000+)	31	56

*Rejections by examining physicians plus Pension Bureau reversals of physician-approved applications.

as the caseload of the pension system became ever larger, reporting for each hundred new applications the number rejected by either examining physicians or Bureau reviewers. There is no evidence of racial discrimination while the annual caseload remained below 50,000; indeed, fewer black applicants were rejected than were whites. As the arrears law prompted more applications in the early 1880s, however, evaluators abruptly changed course and settled into a new behavior that lasted through the remainder of the general-law period and continued under the disability law. No longer did officials favor African-American applicants: instead, evaluators consistently rejected roughly twenty-five more black applicants than whites per hundred.[33]

This pattern shift did not result from a change in applicants' qualifications. White and black applicants were equally in possession of a hospital record through 1880 (91 percent for whites and 94 percent for African Americans), and again afterward (74 percent for both races for the rest of the general-law period). Nor was the shift occasioned by a change in key decision makers: Thomas B. Hood, the referee who oversaw pension ratings made by the medical staff, held the office from the early 1870s until the mid-1880s. Nor, finally, did the shift stem from revelations about race-based application fraud. To be sure, the Pension Bureau did investigate reports of wrongdoing in the South, concluding that African-American applicants and pensioners had been caught up in "systematic extortion and fraud." Yet this scheme was discovered in 1870, and pension evaluators continued to treat the races equitably for another decade.[34]

Though the pension system's caseload rose steadily, Table 3–7 shows that racial discrimination materialized across a threshold and thereafter remained relatively stable in the face of changing pension laws, shifting partisan politics, and nationally escalating racism. We can know little about physicians' and administrators' racial attitudes, but it is doubtful that around 1881 they developed a sudden mistrust of African Americans. It is more likely that through the 1870s, the volume of applications allowed evaluators to treat applicants more or less as individuals; as the annual caseload jumped past 50,000, and then past 100,000 and 200,000, no one could give applicants more than cursory attention, inviting substitution of long-standing racial prejudice for time-consuming investigation of pension worthiness.

Decisions to recommend or deny pensions rested partly on conceptions of disability held by applicants and administrators. We have already noted a racial difference in the prevalence of wounds and service-related illnesses among Civil War survivors, and differing official reactions to mental and other disabilities; it is equally important to explore additional patterns in pension-seekers' presentation and administrators' evaluation of disabilities.

Pension legislation may have devoted more attention to battle wounds than to diseases, but army life accomplished the opposite. Military hospitals treated well over 1.5 million cases of diarrhea among white soldiers and more than 150,000 among African Americans, six times the number of reported wounds. Veterans continued to complain about diarrhea's lingering effects, but this malady was eventually overtaken by the infirmities of aging, especially rheumatism. The latter collection of debilities, including arthritis and other problems of the muscles and joints, became the most frequently occurring condition cited in pension applications from both races. Table 3–8 ranks these diseases and the three other leading disabilities cited in first applications by each race in each pension-law period, along with examining physicians' and the Pension Bureau's acceptance of claims for each disability. For comparison with a "stigmatized" disability, the table also includes claims of mental illness.[35]

Table 3-8 *Applicants', examining physicians', and Pension Bureau's ranking of leading disabilities plus mental illness in first applications, CPE samples*

A. Whites under General Law

By Applicants (% of 11,658 Applications)	By Physicians (% Recommended)	By Bureau (% Recommendations Approved)
Diarrhea (24)	Wounds (51)	Diarrhea (73)
Wounds (21)	Rheumatism (44)	Wounds (57)
Rheumatism (19)	Respiratory (38)	Rheumatism (48)
Respiratory (12)	Diarrhea (38)	Respiratory (41)
Heart (7)	Heart (31)	Heart (23)
Mental Illness (3)	Mental Illness (22)	Mental Illness (15)

B. African Americans under General Law

By Applicants (% of 783 Applications)	By Physicians (% Recommended)	By Bureau (% Recommendations Approved)
Wounds (28)	Wounds (65)	Diarrhea (47)
Rheumatism (27)	Rheumatism (42)	Wounds (43)
Diarrhea (12)	Respiratory (36)	Respiratory (36)
Respiratory (8)	Diarrhea (19)	Rheumatism (24)
Heart (3)	Heart (8)	Heart (4)
Mental Illness (1)	Mental Illness (0)	Mental Illness (0)

C. Whites under Disability Law

By Applicants (% of 6,345 Applications)	By Physicians (% Recommended)	By Bureau (% Recommendations Approved)
Rheumatism (52)	Rheumatism (58)	Rheumatism (55)
Heart (25)	Wounds (57)	Diarrhea (49)
Respiratory (14)	Respiratory (50)	Heart (44)

C. Whites under Disability Law *(cont.)*

By Applicants (% of 6,345 Applications)	By Physicians (% Recommended)	By Bureau (% Recommendations Approved)
Diarrhea (13)	Diarrhea (46)	Respiratory (30)
Mental Illness (6)	Heart (42)	Mental Illness (14)
Wounds (5)	Mental Illness (23)	Wounds (11)

D. African Americans under Disability Law

By Applicants (% of 1,135 Applications)	By Physicians (% Recommended)	By Bureau (% Recommendations Approved)
Rheumatism (61)	Wounds (56)	Diarrhea (53)
Respiratory (15)	Rheumatism (47)	Rheumatism (50)
Heart (14)	Heart (35)	Respiratory (35)
Wounds (11)	Respiratory (29)	Heart (30)
Diarrhea (7)	Mental Illness (17)	Wounds (15)
Mental Illness (5)	Diarrhea (16)	Mental Illness (12)

The table underscores veterans' awareness (and that of the claim houses that helped them) about the law's requirements. Wounds, which were at or near the top of applicants' claims under the general law, dropped to near the bottom after 1890, replaced by claims of rheumatism, which appeared in more than half of disability-law applications. Though both races exhibited this trend, sharp racial differences appear in other diseases reported by applicants and in official evaluations of them. Diarrhea and related intestinal disorders are the key case in point: though such disorders' war-era occurrence was considerably greater among black soldiers, they cited intestinal maladies only half as often as did whites throughout the periods under study. Moreover, physicians accepted African Americans' diarrhea claims only half as often as for white soldiers under the general law, and the rate dropped below even the acceptance of mental-illness claims after 1890. This disparity is probably not the result of simple prejudice on the part of examining physicians: under the general law, they were much more likely to approve African Americans than whites for wound claims, and continued to treat such claims equally under the disability law. The discrepancy between the prevalence of intestinal disorders in the army and black veterans' experience with claims citing these disorders warrants further investigation.[36]

A difference in the meaning of intestinal disorders emerges from analysis of applicants' claims beyond the figures shown in Table 3–8. Among whites who submitted claims citing diarrhea and dysentery, more than half (54 percent) made this the only major disability (defined as the disabilities reported in Table 3–8) in their claim; the corresponding proportion for black applicants is closer to one-third (38 percent). These proportions suggest that white applicants considered intestinal disorders a serious disability, and physicians, as the results shown in Table 3–8 attest, accepted these diseases at rates comparable to other disabilities. African-American veterans, on the other hand, usually combined a diarrhea or dysentery claim with another major disability, presenting examining physicians with more options. The physicians, as we have seen in Table 3–4, accepted at least one disability for most African Americans; when the physicians saw a diarrhea claim for a black applicant, there was usually at least one "real" disability accompanying it, so the typical course was to accept another claim and reject the intestinal disorder. This unwitting collaboration between applicants and evaluators produced a racialized meaning for intestinal disorders: they were legitimate disabilities for white veterans, but black veterans and their examining physicians viewed these diseases with roughly the same disdain as mental illnesses.

The Pension Bureau was the final author of a meaning for disability. The third column of Table 3–8 ranks the Bureau's approvals of physician-endorsed disability claims. For both races, the Bureau's reviewers privileged conditions with plentiful hospital evidence, such as intestinal disorders or the visibly inflamed joints of rheumatism, over maladies that were especially dependent on examining physicians' judgment, such as heart and respiratory diseases. And the Bureau was especially likely to disallow wound claims after 1890 and claims of mental illness whenever they appeared.

Physicians and Bureau reviewers alike had been impressed by wounds under the general law, and examining surgeons continued to accept more than half of such claims after 1890. The Bureau, however, was deeply suspicious of war-era wounds' long-term effect on the ability to work; a pension attorney hinted at official reasoning in his opinion that "gunshot wounds in nine cases out of ten get better with the lapse of time," especially when the veteran was "able gradually to adapt himself to it." On the other hand, even after examining physicians had rejected four out of five claims of psychological disability, the Bureau's reviewers nonetheless dismissed five-sixths of those that remained, demonstrating the continuing hostility to mental illness as a legitimate disease.[37]

Table 3–8 underscores the Pension Bureau's mistrust of examining physicians' judgment. Throughout the periods observed, the physicians reordered the ranking of disabilities that pension seekers had established, putting wound-related disability at or near the top of the accepted conditions and downgrading intestinal disorders, especially for African Americans. Then, however, the Bureau's reviewers reordered the hierarchy again, restoring intestinal diseases to acceptability under the general law and repeatedly disallowing claims after 1890 that involved war-era wounds.

Two struggles over the meaning of disability thus unfolded, both involving race. One struggle contested the causes of disability, working to black veterans' disadvantage insofar as they declined to pursue claims involving intestinal disorders. The second struggle concerned consequences, that is, the current inability "to earn a support." Tables 3–4 through 3–6 indicate that whatever the asserted cause, and regardless of examining physicians' judgment, Pension-Bureau reviewers were disproportionately skeptical of black applicants' claims that they were unable to support themselves.

Race clearly mattered in the Civil War pension system. It mattered to Clay Ballard because he said so, but it also made a tangible difference in the lives of other African Americans who were rejected for a pension: previous research has indicated that federal pensions enabled recipients to live longer than nonpensioners. Yet we also suggested in Chapter 1 that race was more than a category of victimization – it was also a spur to assertion of manhood. Circumstantial evidence of such assertiveness emerged in the 1890s, when African-American pension applications outpaced those from whites, and other evidence appears in the statements that veterans made about themselves when they appeared before the examining physicians.[38]

These statements, which began the physical examination, were mediated narratives of the applicant's condition. Transcribed by the physician designated as secretary, sometimes in summary form and sometimes verbatim, the statements may also have been shaped by claim-house coaching. Nonetheless, contrasting patterns appear in the statements of white and black pension seekers.

Whites could be remarkably candid about their diminished manhood: one veteran admitted that "now I am no man at all. ... My l[eft] leg is practically useless and I would be much better if it were cut off," and another complained that he had "never been a man" since a wound to his hips and back. Some whites acknowledged lost strength and productivity ("I am broke down generally," "I am a wreck," "He claims he is nervous and broke down"), while others expressed their condition as fractions of "a man" ("Am not half the man I was," "I am perhaps half a man at manual labor," "I am just about half a man taken on an average").[39]

These admissions may be unremarkable from men seeking a pension, but they are essentially missing from the statements of African-American applicants. A few black veterans referred to the effects of age ("I am an old man and can do no work"), and one applicant admitted that he was "about half of a hand at labor," but he added that he was also "a man of temperate habits." None of the black applicants in the CPE samples used the "broken down" or "half a man" phrasing, nor did they echo the whites' more direct acknowledgment of lost manly traits. Unlike the measures of significance reflected in this chapter's tables, there is nothing to tell us whether other samples of pension records would differ from these statements in the CPE samples. The patterns in the sample statements accord with African Americans' participation under the disability law, however, in suggesting that black veterans considered claiming a pension as an assertion of manhood.[40]

For the men who passed judgment on these veterans, the concept of race was the ideal economizer: by ruling out uncertainty and eliminating the need for reflection and further investigation, race provided a widely understood explanation of character and motivation. For all its apparent rigidity, however, race was not an absolute barrier between worthiness and unworthiness for a pension. When black veterans such as Levi Showell presented clearly incapacitating wounds, there was no doubt about their eligibility for a pension; Showell began receiving payments for his shoulder wound in 1866. In cases calling for administrative discretion, such as those of Clay Ballard and Willis Pleasant, race became an attractive tool for cutting through uncertainty.[41]

Race was thus a lifeline to examining physicians, offering a simple formulation to cope with an increasingly onerous round of examinations, and to Pension-Bureau reviewers facing an even greater caseload. Race likewise offered the Bureau's officials the satisfaction of imposing a measure of order on a system, the operation of which was largely beyond their control. Ethnicity could also have shaped the experience of pension seekers and the behavior of government officials; Chapter 4 investigates the effects of ethnic background on the functioning of the pension system.

4

Pensions for Foreign-Born Veterans

T he state of knowledge regarding foreign-born
soldiers and veterans of the Civil War differs from
what is known about African Americans. Studies of
the wartime experiences of immigrants to the North typically focus on "ethnic units," those regiments and brigades
with significant representation of an immigrant group. This
approach is sensible because the companies that made up
army regiments, recruited from towns and neighborhoods,
should have reflected the community life that characterized
the immigrant experience.[1]

Yet the transfer of ethnic communities to the army
must be considered in its context. Taking the two largest
immigrant groups, only 11 percent of Irish-born soldiers
and 18 percent of German Americans in the CPE samples
served in ethnic companies, that is, in which a majority of

their comrades were their countrymen. Accounts of ethnic units cannot fully capture individual soldiers' experiences, especially given the diseases and wounds that shaped the postwar population of disabled veterans.[2]

Likewise, aside from biographies of prominent immigrants who served the Union, few studies illuminate the postwar lives of foreign-born veterans. Thousands of immigrants came home from the Civil War with battle scars or bodies weakened by disease, and it is important to understand how they fared in the federal pension system, particularly in light of the treatment of African Americans described in Chapter 3. This chapter investigates the experience of immigrants with the risks of war and with veterans' benefits after the War's end.[3]

As was the case with African Americans, underlying patterns in disability can be uncovered by pursuing traditional questions about soldiering in the Civil War. Because records of foreign-born soldiers were not segregated in the manner of those for the U.S. Colored Troops, less is known about immigrants' experience with the hazards of war. Previous investigations of battlefield conduct and ethnic character, however, are a useful starting point for exploring the distinctiveness of immigrants' life in the army.[4]

As battles became increasingly bloody in the War's second year, Irish units took particularly heavy casualties. The Battle of Fredericksburg in December of 1862 emerged as the icon of Irish bloodshed, with two important consequences. An already skeptical Irish-American populace became convinced that Irish lives were being disproportionately sacrificed for the Union, a belief that contributed to draft riots on the home front and desertion and declining enlistments in the army. Second, Fredericksburg's chroniclers labored to make the battle a testament to the superiority of the Irish-born soldier: participation in a doomed assault on fortified positions became a demonstration of Irish patriotism and courage.[5]

The combat performance of German-born soldiers also became a significant wartime issue. Many Germans served with distinction, but as with the Irish, German Americans' conduct was epitomized by one battle. Left unprotected against a flanking attack at the Battle of Chancellorsville in May of 1863, the Army of the Potomac's Eleventh Corps was overrun by Stonewall Jackson's troops. The Eleventh included a substantial number of German Americans, many of whom valiantly resisted the assault. Reports of German courage, however, were overshadowed by charges that the defeat at Chancellorsville was due to "the disgraceful flight of the flying Dutchmen." These accusations were amplified by newspaper accounts into a stereotype of the shirking German soldier. Resentment of the stereotype contributed to a disaffection from the Northern cause that paralleled the post-Fredericksburg alienation of the Irish, but German Americans lacked mythmakers to transfigure their experiences in the style of the Irish Brigade.[6]

These issues of ethnicity and combat performance are important to the present study for two reasons. First, investigating wartime disability, specifically in the form of wounds, reveals patterns in the evolution of ethnicity as a concept. In both the Irish and German cases, critics and apologists struggled over the fundamental source of supposed differences in ethnic behavior and experience. When immigrant advocates warned of alienation from the Union cause, they insisted that the fault was institutional. Accusing the army of systematically mishandling immigrants, a Boston newspaper declared that the Irish-born soldier was "being reduced to dust and being made food for gunpowder," and a speaker at a German-American rally denounced the "cry of slander against the German rank and file," which "must inevitably chill the enthusiasm of the German population."[7]

On the other hand, those who lionized the Irish at Fredericksburg, and those who vilified German-born soldiers at Chancellorsville, implied that combat performance originated in individual character traits. A writer insisted that "the Irish soldier has won a high reputation" and that few "question his bravery as a soldier or his devotion to the flag under which he fought," and a journalist reported that Germans were known for "slinging down their arms, running away, or surrendering themselves to the enemy when there was the slightest danger."[8]

A second reason for exploring ethnicity and battlefield conduct is the issue's postwar implications. If the risks of combat fell differently on different immigrant groups, the disparity would be reflected in the population of disabled

Table 4-1 *Percent of white CPE sample members hospitalized for a wound, by country of birth*

Country of Birth	% Wounded
United States	18.0
Germany	14.7
Ireland	21.7
Other	16.4
Number of cases	33,469

veterans that is this study's central interest. The toll of these risks on members of the CPE samples is thus the starting point for this chapter's analyses.

Table 4–1 shows the percentage of white CPE sample members who suffered at least one wound during the Civil War. The figures appear to confirm contemporary stereotypes: German-born soldiers were least likely and Irish soldiers most likely to be wounded. These rates, however, could have been the product of soldiers' other characteristics, and Table 4–2 pursues various explanations for the toll of combat. Focusing on whites in the CPE samples, the table gauges individual (age, occupation at enlistment, noncommissioned rank, and nationality) and institutional (presence at major battles and the percentage of countrymen in each sample member's company) influences on the risk of being wounded.[9]

Age and class helped to shape soldiers' combat experience. The Civil War gave young men ample opportunity to display their sense of invulnerability: one commander

Table 4–2 *Comparative risk of receiving a battle wound, whites in CPE samples*

Variable	Mean	Hazard Ratio
Age at enlistment	24.9	**.99**
Noncommissioned officer	.143	**1.33**
White-collar occupation at enlistment	.060	.77
Irish born	.078	**1.26**
Percent of company Irish born	8.5	**1.01**
German born	.066	1.12
Percent of company German born	7.2	1.00
Other immigrant	.087	1.08
With company at		
Antietam	.004	**3.25**
Fredericksburg	.009	**1.87**
Chancellorsville	.012	**2.60**
Gettysburg	.011	**2.87**
Number of cases		29,601

Note: Hazard ratios in boldface indicate $p < .05$

reported that "two of the youngest soldiers bearing arms in the regiment … stood in a most exposed position … firing deliberately" during the Battle of Seven Pines. Table 4–2 shows the wages of youthful bravado versus maturer caution – the older the soldier, the less likely he was to suffer a battle wound.[10]

Soldiers who had had white-collar occupations before the War (clerk, merchant, student, and the like) were also less likely to be wounded. Whether they benefitted from prudence or shirking is unclear, but avoiding shot and shell may have contributed to the occasional ridicule of the "paper-collar young man" and "high-toned recruits." Noncommissioned rank, on the other hand, aggravated the risks of battle: leaders and exhorters, especially when they were color bearers, faced dangers that are reflected in their increased odds of being wounded.[11]

Table 4–2 also reveals important collective effects on battlefield risks. Major engagements took their grim toll on all participants, but there remained a strong, collective "Irish" impact on casualties – the more Irish the company, the greater the likelihood of a member's being wounded. This heightened risk applied to everyone, Irish born or not, in Irish units; on the other hand, the essential irrelevance of German birth and German comrades accords with recent judgments that condemnation of German-born soldiers after Chancellorsville is unwarranted. Commanders either consistently put Irish units in harm's way or Irish troops' bravery inspired everyone, Irishmen and others alike, to throw caution aside.[12]

Disease was the other scourge of the Civil War, killing more soldiers than did battle wounds. Ethnic differences in the occurrence of disease would also shape the postwar disabled population, so we begin with an assertion about disease by the German-born soldier Henry Kircher.

Serving in a largely German regiment from Missouri, Kircher wrote that "regiments consisting mostly of Germans have better health than those consisting of Americans or Irish," because the German diet was better and because "cleanliness is also much more in fashion among the Germans than in the other regiments." As with contemporary assertions about combat performance, this claim proves nothing, but it provides an expectation that can be tested.[13]

Table 4–3 reports hospitalization for one or more serious illnesses among native-born and immigrant soldiers in the CPE samples. The results suggest that Henry Kircher was both right and wrong in his assertions: German-born soldiers in the CPE samples were less likely to contract a serious illness than were the native born, but disease incidence among the Irish was similarly low. To explore reasons for these differences, Table 4–4 investigates variables that might have made soldiers more or less susceptible to illnesses. In addition to straightforward characteristics such as age, occupation, place of birth, and military rank, the table also includes variables for surviving disease exposure in a large city and for service in disease-ridden areas outside the Eastern theater. In view of the contagiousness of many Civil War ailments, and Henry Kircher's assertions about company composition, the table assigns each soldier the percentage of German and Irish comrades in his company.[14]

The hazard ratios in Table 4–4 underscore the importance of age and exposure to disease. Older men were more susceptible to serious illness, and those who served in the Gulf states and the West clearly shared the miseries of the Ninth Connecticut Infantry, which saw 153 men contract diseases in one month near Vicksburg. Class, as indicated by a white-collar occupation before enlistment,

Table 4–3 *Percent of white CPE sample members hospitalized for a "severe," "acute," or "chronic" illness while in the army, whites in CPE samples*

Country of Birth	% Ill
United States	13.0
Germany	7.2
Ireland	6.9
Other	10.1
Number of cases	33,469

Table 4–4 *Comparative risk of being hospitalized for a "severe," "acute," or "chronic" illness while in the army, whites in CPE samples*

Variable	Mean	Hazard ratio
Age at enlistment	24.9	**1.028**
White-collar occupation at enlistment	.061	.885
Enlisted in city of 30,000 or more	.188	**.699**
Noncommissioned officer	.141	.953
First service outside Eastern theater	.541	**1.403**
Born in Germany	.068	.862
Born in Ireland	.080	**.719**
Other foreign birth	.086	.988
Percent of company German born	6.8	**.985**
Percent of company Irish born	8.0	**.995**
Number of cases	29,601	

Note: Hazard ratios in boldface indicate $p < .05$

made no appreciable difference in the risk of disease, nor did noncommissioned officers' segregation from the crowded quarters occupied by privates. On the other hand, men who enlisted in cities had already been exposed to the pathogens that thrived in crowded conditions, which lessened their disease risk by nearly one-third compared to their rural comrades.[15]

With these circumstances controlled, distinctive ethnic influences remain, again confirming and modifying Henry Kircher's claims. Irishmen, but not Germans or other immigrants, enjoyed better health no matter where they served, but there was also a collective disease differential: the more German- or Irish-born soldiers there were in a company, the less likely any comrade was to suffer a serious illness. Probing more deeply into the causes of these distinctions is beyond the scope of this study, but the disease results are additional evidence for ethnic differences that potentially affected pension eligibility. Veterans who had served in Irish companies were especially likely to bear the scars of wartime wounds, while they and those who served with German Americans were less likely to have records of confinement for a disease that could substantiate a pension claim.

Despite the differences in disabling conditions among immigrants and natives, in principle all veterans had access to the same system of Civil War benefits. We might predict that foreign-born veterans would shy away from pensions: limited English would deter some from the complex application process, and those who were literate might read comments by the prominent pension attorney and lobbyist George E. Lemon, who denounced "the hordes of ignorant Poles, Hungarians, Russian Jews, and Italians which the cupidity of steamship lines is dumping on our shores." On the other hand, the Irish, with their disproportionate wounds, might be expected to be eager pension seekers, and nativist invective often exempted Civil War veterans. Lemon, for example, emphasized that all veterans had "been comrades in a mighty struggle for the preservation of the Nation's existence," and their comradeship united "Native and foreign born, Catholic and Protestant, Jew and Catholic, black and white." Were foreign-born veterans discouraged from seeking a pension, or were men who had been motivated to fight for their new nation also moved to assert their pension rights?[16]

Table 4–5 shows first-pension application rates by country of birth for the first two pension-law periods. As with African Americans, foreign-born veterans were underrepresented among general-law applicants; after mid-1890, again resembling black veterans, ethnic differences disappeared, as nearly all surviving foreign-born veterans sought a pension. To investigate reasons for immigrants' early reluctance to apply, Table 4–6 analyzes the likelihood of a first pension application under the general law. The three immigrant groups that have appeared in earlier tables are again the central interest, but additional variables control for wartime influences that conceivably influenced veterans' willingness to seek a pension.

Table 4–5 *Percent of Civil War survivors who applied for a new pension by country of birth, whites in CPE samples*

Country of Birth	1862–1890	1890–1907
United States	47.2	91.6
Germany	34.8	92.1
Ireland	31.5	89.6
Other	37.0	92.9
Number of cases	25,158	6,767

In addition to hospitalization for a wound or an illness, Table 4–6 gauges the effect of enlistment as a substitute. Fewer than 5 percent of native-born men served as substitutes, but more than 15 percent of foreign-born recruits did so. Wartime ostracism might have discouraged substitutes from seeking pensions afterward: a former officer in the New Hampshire infantry declared, for example, that substitutes "represented the lowest class of almost every nationality," and the presence of "such vile rubbish" was "a desecration of the memory of [soldiers'] late comrades."[17]

Table 4–6 is divided into separate analyses for the periods before and after the arrears law of 1879, because some variables' effects change markedly under the amended regulations. The hazard ratios indicate that veterans with war wounds were especially likely to apply in the early years of the pension system, and that service as a substitute was indeed a consistent deterrent to pension seeking. The most striking change between periods is the behavior of German-born veterans, who, even when they had been wounded or

Table 4–6 *Comparative likelihood of applying for a new pension before mid-1890, whites in CPE samples*

A. *Including Country of Birth*

Variable	1862–1879		1879–1890	
	Mean	Hazard Ratio	Mean	Hazard Ratio
Hospitalized for wound	.287	**4.913**	.240	**1.491**
Hospitalized for illness	.676	**1.453**	.678	**2.371**
Enlisted as substitute	.059	**.439**	.063	**.552**
Born in Germany	.073	**.657**	.068	.998
Born in Ireland	.076	.951	.053	**.834**
Other foreign birth	.092	**.873**	.085	.935
Number of cases	25,160		16,451	

B. *Birthplace Classified by Language*

Variable	1862–1879		1879–1890	
	Mean	Hazard Ratio	Mean	Hazard Ratio
Hospitalized for wound	.287	**4.90**	.240	**1.48**
Hospitalized for illness	.676	**1.46**	.678	**2.37**
Enlisted as substitute	.059	**.431**	.063	**.544**
Born in non-English-speaking country	.090	**.664**	.091	.972
Number of cases	25,160		16,451	

Note: Hazard ratios in boldface indicate $p < .05$

contracted an illness, were one-third less likely than native-born veterans to apply before the arrears law, only to catch up in the next decade.

The behavior of Irish-born veterans, whose propensity to apply is indistinguishable from natives' before 1879, suggests an explanation for the German anomaly. Part B of Table 4–6 reclassifies veterans based on the language of their country of birth. The resulting analysis shows that immigrants from other non-English-speaking countries shared in Germans' behavior – other characteristics being equal, all were one-third less likely than native English-speakers to apply, a difference that disappeared after passage of the arrears law.

These results hint at the importance of publicity in stimulating awareness of pensions. English-language newspapers and magazines routinely reported on pension availability and changes in legislation; it is beyond this study's scope to investigate pension coverage in the foreign-language press, but we do know that pension publicity in general flourished in the wake of the arrears law. Leading the way in this surge of publicity were pension attorneys and their new publications aimed at attracting applicants (and fees), and a reinvigorated Grand Army of the Republic advocating pensions in the drive for members and political influence. The role of the foreign-language press in publicizing Union army pensions remains to be studied, but the surge of interest by veterans from non-English-speaking countries suggests a campaign for awareness in multiple languages.[18]

These results, taken together with the findings of Chapter 3, suggest that initial access to the pension system was constrained by ethnicity as well as by race, but they also indicate that failure to apply arose from varying sources. Veterans from non-English-speaking countries were less handicapped by the poverty, illiteracy, and poor health that plagued many black veterans. Non-English-speaking immigrants who appeared in the 1870 census were more literate and wealthier than those from English-speaking nations, and their health, based on death rates in the CPE samples, was better. Lower participation in the pension system by African Americans and immigrants, though it contributed to making the system disproportionately white and native born, was rooted in distinctive causes and continued for differing periods of time.[19]

Chapter 3 described examining physicians' discrimination against black applicants, followed by a more substantial bias on the part of Pension Bureau reviewers. Physicians could be sympathetic in their face-to-face encounters with immigrants: when George Fichter, a French-born veteran who had been wounded in the siege of Fort Donelson in 1862, requested an increased general-law pension, an examining physician admitted that "I know of no reason for an increase." Nonetheless, because Fichter had recently endured flooding in New Orleans and because "he appears destitute and not able to work," the physician recommended an increase from $10 to $12 a month; Pension Bureau reviewers, however, were unmoved and rejected the change. Were Fichter and other immigrants systematically treated differently from their native-born comrades?[20]

The dominant feature in much of Table 4–7, which displays the results of first applications for a pension among CPE sample members, is uniformity. Both examining physicians and the Pension Bureau consistently approved approximately three-quarters of all applicants under the general law. The physicians raised their approvals to 90 percent under the disability law, still with little ethnic distinction. An apparent bias does appear, however, in the actions of Pension Bureau reviewers under the later law: the Bureau continued to approve approximately three-quarters of applications from native-born and German veterans, but approval rates for immigrants from Ireland and elsewhere dropped to two-thirds.

Table 4–8 investigates this change in Pension Bureau behavior by estimating influences on the odds of reversal of physicians' recommendations for a disability-law pension. The table includes variables that might have produced an apparent ethnic bias – non-German immigrants, for example, were somewhat less likely to apply during the lenient Harrison administration – and an ethnic classification suggested by Table 4–7 and contemporary developments.

As a hierarchy of white "races" became increasingly recognized in the late nineteenth century, the sharpest dividing line formed between a superior category, variously labeled "Anglo-Saxon," "Nordic," and "old stock," versus a conglomerate of "inferior" races. The superior race's

Table 4-7 *Examining physicians' pension recommendations and Pension Bureau awards by country of birth, white applicants for new pensions in CPE samples*

A. Physicians' Recommendations

	1862–1890	1890–1907
Percent of U.S.-born applicants recommended for a pension	74.6	90.9
Percent of German-born applicants recommended for a pension	72.7	90.9
Percent of Irish-born applicants recommended for a pension	76.5	85.7
Percent of other immigrants recommended for a pension	79.1	88.0
Number of examinations	7,705	5,659

B. Pension Bureau Awards

Percent of U.S.-born applicants awarded a pension	78.3	72.9
Percent of German-born applicants awarded a pension	73.4	76.0
Percent of Irish-born applicants awarded a pension	77.8	67.2
Percent of other immigrants awarded a pension	76.6	67.6
Number of rulings	7,530	5,479

origins were typically traced to "British, German, and Scandinavian stock, historically free, energetic, [and] progressive," whereas lower orders such as the "Slav, Latin, and Asiatic" were "historically downtrodden, atavistic, and stagnant." The "Celtic" race to which the Irish belonged

Table 4–8 *Comparative odds of Pension Bureau reversal, first-time white applicants in CPE samples who had been approved by examining physicians, 1890–1907*

Variable	Mean	Odds ratio
Age	56.4	**.979**
Noncommissioned officer	.063	1.030
Assisted by claim house	.886	.995
Examined in Harrison's term	.775	**.523**
Examined in Cleveland's second term	.052	1.261
Number of disabilities claimed	3.60	**.831**
Claims included mental illness	.061	**1.334**
Applicant asserted inability for manual labor	.084	.891
Immigrant from "Anglo-Saxon" nation	.118	.961
Immigrant from elsewhere	.082	**1.338**
Number of applicants	4,910	

Note: Odds ratios in boldface indicate $p < .05$

was occasionally included in the superior group, but was more often denigrated for its alleged inferior qualities. "The Celt," wrote one commentator, "is fundamentally different from the Anglo-Saxon," because the former "lacks the solidity, the balance, the judgment, the moral staying power of the Anglo-Saxon." Immigrants in Table 4–8 are thus divided into two groups: those from Britain, Germany, and the Scandinavian countries who were recognized as "Anglo-Saxon," versus other immigrants relegated to the various "downtrodden" races.[21]

THE HIGH TIDE OF IMMIGRATION—A NATIONAL MENACE.

The "national menace" of turn-of-the-century immigration, consisting of non-"Anglo-Saxon" swimmers labeled "Mafia," "Illiterate," "Pauper," and the like. (*Judge* magazine, 1903)

Table 4–8 finds many of the influences on Pension Bureau reviewers that were discussed in Chapter 3 – they were impressed by the number of conditions cited but not by veterans' own diagnoses of their work disability or by claim-house assistance, they were hostile to claims that included mental illness, and they consistently followed commitments to leniency during the Harrison administration and policies on age eligibility afterward. At the same time, however, the Bureau apparently began to apply ethnic criteria to applicants' credibility. Pension seekers' place of birth often appeared in records sent by the War Department, and unfamiliar names were additional evidence of ethnicity at a time of heightened sensitivity to "inferior" immigrants. With other characteristics of the veteran and his physician-approved application equal, Pension-Bureau reviewers judged applications from "Anglo-Saxon" immigrants essentially the same as those from native-born veterans, but the reviewers were one-third more likely to reject an applicant who belonged to a "downtrodden" race.

Pension officials viewed their mission as extracting order from a system that teemed with disorder. In the eyes of the Bureau, veterans sought pensions without knowing what was expected of them; claim houses advocated cases they knew were fraudulent; members of Congress continually disrupted the Bureau's work with inquiries about claims; physicians, according to a medical referee, "really [do] not understand how to make the rating properly"; and the law itself was a source of disorder. The same referee declared that "the method of rating disabilities is exceedingly complicated. It is not by any means an easy matter to take up the law and then proceed to examine an applicant and decide that he is entitled to such and such a pension." Yet by insisting on compliance and credibility, the Bureau could manufacture a product, the final "rating," that would embody its commitment to regularity and uniformity.[22]

This all-important product required a final judgment on the completed application. Two consecutive physician-approved applications with equivalent details (i.e., equivalent compliance with procedures) should have produced the same result, even if one applicant was born in Sweden and the other in Hungary. Because credibility was crucial, however, the Bureau had additional judging to do. If the two examining boards' medical diagnoses were equally credible, the work-disability consequences still required adjudication. The Bureau relied on evidence that the examining physicians had not seen, including "the testimony of the man's family physician and his neighbors who see him in daily life." Much of this testimony came from friends, neighbors, and relatives of the same nationality as the applicant, and their signatures carried the same credibility as the birthplace on the applicant's military record. Because the latest "scientific" theories held that some "races" were less trustworthy than others, the Swedish applicant had better odds of a final approval than did the Hungarian veteran; this result was repeated often enough to produce the statistics of Table 4–8.[23]

The emergence of this ethnic discrimination had little to do with the volume of applications, another cause of disorder for pension reviewers. We suggested in Chapter 3 that the onset of discrimination against black applicants in the early 1880s is better explained by a surge in the application caseload than by a sudden discovery of prejudice against African Americans. Table 4–9, on the other hand, compares rejected applications in the same way as Table 3–7, and points to just such a discovery regarding immigrants. The table shows that native whites and immigrants received roughly equal treatment from evaluators long after they had turned against black applicants. This would appear to contradict

Table 4–9 *Place of Birth, pension rejections, and the application caseload*

| Period (Annual Caseload) | Rejections per 100 New Applications in CPE Samples* | | |
	Native-Born Applicants	Applicants from "Anglo-Saxon" Nations	Applicants Born Elsewhere
1862–1880 (under 50,000)	35	40	33
1881–1882 (50,000–100,000)	42	44	43
1883–1889 (100,000–200,000)	35	39	33
1890–1907 (200,000+)	30	30	46

* Rejections by examining physicians plus Pension Bureau reversals of physician-approved applications.

the connection between the caseload and discrimination, but the chronology of racial prejudice suggests otherwise. Compared with the longstanding animus against African Americans, prejudice against "downtrodden races" was very much a late nineteenth-century discovery. Combining existing racial prejudice and contemporary fascination with scientific explanations, it prescribed an appropriate response to the "new" immigration. If the rise of discrimination against black applicants was a case of using an old tool to handle a new workload, discrimination against certain immigrants represents a new tool used against a new threat to American "racial integrity."

In Chapter 3 we saw considerable racial variation in presentation of disabilities by applicants and evaluation by physicians and the Pension Bureau. Table 4–10, which replicates
the classification of claims in Chapter 3, reveals smaller differences between immigrants and native-born whites. The
only substantial distinction in disability claims was the less-
frequent mention of diarrhea by foreign-born applicants,
especially under the general law, undoubtedly reflecting
the smaller likelihood of disease among immigrants shown
in Table 4–2. Official approvals were also similar between
immigrants and natives, with only the response to mental
claims showing a noteworthy difference. As we have seen in
Table 4–8, Pension Bureau reviewers were especially suspicious of mental-illness claims by immigrants under the disability law, but Table 4–10 indicates that physicians were
equally skeptical. Foreign-born veterans were somewhat
less likely than natives to present such claims; when immigrants did allege mental illness, however, physicians were
10 percentage points less likely to accept the claims than
with native-born applicants, and the Pension Bureau was 10
percentage points less likely to add its approval.

Otherwise, the bias against some immigrants that
appears in Tables 4–7 and 4–8 had few consequences in
acceptance of disability; differential approvals were thus
spread through the leading conditions shown in Table 4–10,
as well as other disabilities that did not qualify for inclusion
in the table. The notable difference in mental illness,
however – the disability category often associated with

Table 4–10 *Applicants', examining physicians', and Pension Bureau's ranking of "Top-5" disabilities plus mental illness, first applications, CPE Samples*

A. Native-Born Whites under General Law

By Applicants (% of 9,255 Applications)	By Physicians (% Recommended)	By Bureau (% Recommendations Approved)
Diarrhea (23)	Wounds (50)	Diarrhea (72)
Wounds (22)	Rheumatism (44)	Wounds (56)
Rheumatism (19)	Respiratory (39)	Rheumatism (47)
Respiratory (12)	Diarrhea (38)	Respiratory (42)
Heart (7)	Heart (32)	Heart (24)
Mental Illness (3)	Mental Illness (20)	Mental Illness (15)

B. Immigrants under General Law

By Applicants (% of 2,170 Applications)	By Physicians (% Recommended)	By Bureau (% Recommendations Approved)
Wounds (31)	Wounds (55)	Diarrhea (73)
Rheumatism (21)	Rheumatism (45)	Wounds (60)
Diarrhea (15)	Diarrhea (35)	Rheumatism (50)
Respiratory (9)	Respiratory (33)	Respiratory (36)
Heart (6)	Heart (26)	Heart (21)
Mental Illness (3)	Mental Illness (25)	Mental Illness (18)

C. Native-Born Whites under Disability Law

By Applicants (% of 4,942 Applications)	By Physicians (% Recommended)	By Bureau (% Recommendations Approved)
Rheumatism (51)	Rheumatism (58)	Rheumatism (55)
Heart (25)	Wounds (56)	Diarrhea (49)

c. Native-Born Whites under Disability Law (Cont.)

By Applicants (% of 4,942 Applications)	By Physicians (% Recommended)	By Bureau (% Recommendations Approved)
Respiratory (15)	Respiratory (49)	Heart (44)
Diarrhea (14)	Diarrhea (46)	Respiratory (30)
Mental Illness (7)	Heart (43)	Mental Illness (16)
Wounds (4)	Mental Illness (25)	Wounds (10)

D. Immigrants under Disability Law

By Applicants (% of 1,313 Applications)	By Physicians (% Recommended)	By Bureau (% Recommendations Approved)
Rheumatism (57)	Wounds (61)	Rheumatism (55)
Heart (22)	Rheumatism (56)	Diarrhea (48)
Respiratory (14)	Respiratory (52)	Heart (41)
Diarrhea (9)	Diarrhea (48)	Respiratory (30)
Wounds (7)	Heart (39)	Wounds (16)
Mental Illness (6)	Mental Illness (14)	Mental Illness (6)

"cheaters" – accords with the late-nineteenth-century fixation on the supposed character deficiencies of "degraded" races.

Foreign-born Civil War veterans should have had little to prove to their adopted nation. They came to America long before the new immigration that so alarmed nativists, and they demonstrated their loyalty by fighting for, and in the case of the Irish, being disproportionately wounded for, their government. Yet foreign-born veterans could hardly escape the implications of "scientific" theories about ethnicity and character. We observed in Chapter 1 that denigration of "downtrodden" men implied belittling their manhood, and we suggested that claiming a pension implied an affirmation of manliness. Immigrants left less testimony to this effect than did African Americans: in their statements to examining physicians, foreign-born veterans were about as likely as natives to admit that they were "broken down" or to evaluate themselves as fractions "of a man." On the other hand, immigrants' insistence on seeking pensions, especially their nearly universal application rates under the disability law, is entirely consistent with a pointed reminder of manly self-sacrifice.

Nonetheless, the pension system put obstacles in the way of foreign-born immigrants' full inclusion as Americans. For reasons that may have included an absence of foreign-language publicity about Civil War pensions, some immigrants failed to apply in the pension system's early years; when the disability law allowed them to qualify for current disabilities, the Pension Bureau disproportionately rejected claims from non-Anglo-Saxon applicants.

The gaps between immigrants and natives in their propensity to apply for pensions and their experiences as applicants were consistently smaller than the difference between African Americans and whites. Yet the increasing racialization of ethnicity and the emergence of nativist prejudice among Pension Bureau administrators brought African Americans and immigrants into a kind of conceptual alignment, uncovering a crucial flaw in a system that ostensibly relied on the individual to prove his worthiness: it was a short step from evaluation of an applicant's character to ascription of assumed group characteristics to the individual.

The ascription might stem from ingrained bias against African Americans or from fashions of the moment, especially mistrust of foreign "races" that had not heretofore been problematic. As long as pension policy was founded on exclusion of the unworthy, and as long as worthiness was in turn rooted in credibility, *a priori* judgments of character would inevitably influence decisions about who would receive pensions.

5

"A More Infamous Gang of Cut-Throats Never Lived"

We have described Civil War pensions as a *system,* to convey the variety of actors who shaped veterans' benefits. Applicants, examining physicians, Pension Bureau reviewers, and inquisitive members of Congress all influenced the pension process, but no participants aroused more controversy than did pension attorneys and their claim houses.

George E. Lemon, Nathan W. Fitzgerald, and Milo B. Stevens do not trigger immediate recognition, even among those knowledgeable about Gilded-Age figures. These attorneys operated pension claim houses that played an important but often-neglected role in the rise of the

The title of the chapter is a speech by John F. Benjamin, in *Congressional Globe*, 41st Cong., 2nd sess., 1967.

bureaucratic state and the legal profession. In addition to running highly lucrative businesses – Lemon's claim house was the largest corporation of its time in Washington, D.C. – pension attorneys functioned as influential lobbyists, tirelessly promoting expanded pensions for all Union army veterans.[1]

For a legislatively regulated fee, claim houses run by Lemon, Fitzgerald, Stevens, and thousands of other ambitious men and women offered assistance to pension seekers. Claim agents typically furnished forms, prepared affidavits, and conducted correspondence with the Pension Bureau on an applicant's behalf. We saw evidence of this assistance in Chapters 3 and 4: claim-house help raised the odds of an applicant's success under the general law, convincing some observers that "these claim agents must have their representatives inside the departments." As our earlier discussion suggested, claim agents' effectiveness was more likely due to their ability to satisfy the Pension Bureau's desire for bureaucratic regularity, but fears of a conspiracy attest to claim houses' significance.[2]

Though the owners of the largest claim houses were typically practicing attorneys, in this chapter "pension attorney" and "claim agent" will refer to individuals with a variety of occupations. One investigation found an advertised "attorney" who was by trade a shoemaker; others were hardware dealers, grocers, farmers, a photographer, and a rag-picker. Nonetheless, all fell under the Pension Bureau's regulations for pension attorneys, and as fee-for-service

George E. Lemon, a captain in the 125th New York Volunteers who was wounded at the Battle of Bristoe Station, Virginia, in 1863, owned the largest claim house and published the pension-advocating *National Tribune*. (From Ezra D. Simons, *A Regimental History: The One Hundred and Twenty-Fifth New York Volunteers*. New York: Ezra D. Simons, 1888)

business owners they focused their attention on the twin pillars of their enterprise, price and volume.[3]

Congress established the attorney fee at $5 in the first general pension law, but thereafter, subject to countervailing pressures from claim agents and their critics, lawmakers repeatedly changed the fee's provisions. After raising the fee to $10 in 1864 (but restricting it to successful applications), Congress moved to end claim houses' practice of making cash advances to pensioners in exchange for liens on their payments. Legislation in 1870 raised the allowable attorney fee to $25 (deductible from the first pension payment), but reserved the rest of the payment for pensioners themselves or their legal guardian.[4]

This law also required the Pension Bureau to approve contracts for the increased fees, generating complaints about the Bureau's increased workload and prompting Congress to revisit the issue in 1878. New legislation returned the attorney fee to $10 and ended government deduction from pension payments. This was not entirely a setback for claim houses: they could now impose a fee on all pension applications, not just those that were ultimately approved.[5]

The new provisions, together with the arrears law's enrichment of pension benefits a year later, touched off a scramble among claim houses that threatened the order that the largest firms had imposed. Table 5–1 shows that the three largest claim houses handled nearly one-fourth of all new applications at the time of the 1878 fee law. These firms actually improved their position during the fee-for-all-claims period, but the table's second column shows a trend that some observers found worrisome: the number of new claim houses nearly doubled, causing a supposed deterioration in client representation. The pension commissioner warned that among the new entrants

Table 5-1 *Three largest firms' share of claim-house business, plus new firms entering claim-house market, from first-time applicants in CPE samples*

Period	Top-Three Share	New Firms
1862–1870	8.4%	701
1870–1878	23.8%	301
1878–1884	28.1%	570
1884–1890	14.7%	445

were "many ignorant, unscrupulous, and useless persons, whose only object seems to be, first, to procure applications from soldiers, regardless of merit, to be filed through them, and then, while acting simply as transmitters of the papers, assiduously dun the claimant until the ten-dollar fee is secured, and thereafter practically abandon the case." George E. Lemon, writing in his widely distributed *National Tribune*, agreed, insisting that his firm's "known and proved integrity" was a bulwark against untrustworthy newcomers. In 1884, motivated by widespread dissatisfaction, lawmakers and pension officials collaborated with Lemon to revise the fee system.[6]

Negotiators initially agreed to revert to the outlines of the 1870 law, including a $25 maximum fee to be deducted from the pensioner's first payment. Then Lemon, meeting with House and Senate conferees as they reconciled differing versions of the legislation, persuaded them to retain language that would make the increased fee retroactive to 1878. Armed with contracts stipulated by the new law,

James R. Tanner illustrates the close relationship between government and special interests that fed suspicion of the pension system. A double amputee from his Civil War service, Tanner served briefly as pension commissioner in 1889, resigned to become a pension attorney, and in 1905 was named commander-in-chief of the Grand Army of the Republic. (From James E. Smith, *A Famous Battery and Its Campaigns, 1861–64: The Career of Corporal James Tanner in War and in Peace*. Washington, DC: W. H. Loudermilk, 1892)

pension attorneys could now demand $15 more from applicants with pending claims.[7]

Table 5–1 shows that, although the number of new claim houses dropped under the revised fee law, the dominant firms could not maintain their market domination. Because their client base had been so large under the previous law, however, the largest houses undoubtedly garnered a disproportionate share of the more than 90,000 retroactive contracts negotiated under the new rules.[8]

The $25 maximum fee remained in effect for new applications under the general law. As Congress debated the disability law in 1890, lawmakers anticipated a volume-generated bonanza for claim agents and considered a $5 fee, then raised the final amount to $10 per successful application. After claim houses fought off an attempt to reduce the fee to one dollar, the fee structure remained intact. The service-pension law of 1907 prohibited attorney fees, thereby phasing out agents' income except for applications under prior laws.[9]

Claim agents' efforts to maximize their volume of business, though they caused unending controversy, also encouraged them to reach out to African Americans and immigrants. The sheer number of pension applications generated a massive flow of income: agents collected nearly $50 million in fees from 1862 through the century's end. Claim agents' tactics, which included using local "subagents" to find potential applicants, publishing newspaper advertisements, distributing circulars with clients' testimonials, and Lemon's buying out his chief rival on the eve of the retroactive fee law, prompted a storm of criticism. Editors and government officials described pension attorneys as "sharks," "leeches," "vultures," and "expensive pests"; denounced agents' publications as "lying circulars" in which "apparent anxiety for the soldiers' welfare and appeals to their love of gain were cunningly intermingled"; and accused claim houses of bleeding veterans "of dollar after dollar, leading them on by stimulating promises, until it was found that no more money could be exacted." Undeterred, claim houses continued to cast a wide net for applicants, including foreign-born and African-American veterans.[10]

Table 5–2 uses the CPE samples to examine the results of claim houses' marketing efforts, listing firms that illustrate varying strategies and outcomes. The largest claim houses, relying on national advertising, built clienteles whose racial and ethnic makeup roughly reflected that of the veteran population. At the same time, many smaller firms solicited locally, presumably relying on subagents and local distribution of circulars. William H. Lusk, based in New York City, drew the majority of his claims from foreign-born (mostly Irish) veterans; Augustus P. Lloyd, operating in Baltimore, obtained half his volume from African Americans; and Nathan Bickford, based in Washington, D.C., was the unusual agent whose business significantly crossed racial lines.

CLAIMS! _____ CLAIMS!

This Claim House Estab-
lished in 1865!

GEORGE E. LEMON,

Attorney-at-Law.

OFFICES, 615 Fifteenth St., (Citizens' National Bank.)

WASHINGTON, D.C.

P.O. DRAWER 325

Pensions.

If wounded, injured, or have contracted any disease, however slight the disability, apply at once. Thousands entitled.

Heirs.

Widows, minor children, dependent mothers, fathers, and minor brothers and sisters, in the order named, are entitled.

War of 1812.

All surviving officers and soldiers of this war, whether in the Military or Naval service of the United States, who served fourteen (14) days; or, if in a battle or skirmish, for a less period, and the widows of such who have not remarried, are entitled to a pension of eight dollars a month. Proof of loyalty is no longer required in these claims.

Increase of Pensions.

Pension laws are more liberal now than formerly, and many are now entitled to a higher rate than they receive.

From and after January, 1881, I shall make no charges for my services in claims for increase of pension, where no new disability is alleged, unless successful in procuring the increase.

Restoration to Pension Roll.

Pensioners who have been unjustly dropped from the pension roll, or whose names have been stricken there-from by reason of failure to draw their pension for a period of three years, or by reason of re-enlistment, may have their pensions renewed by corresponding with this house.

Desertion

from one regiment or vessel and enlistment in another is not a bar to pension in cases where the wound, disease, or injury was incurred while in the service of the United States, and in the line of duty.

Land Warrants.

Survivors of all wars from 1790, to March 3, 1866, and certain heirs are entitled to one hundred and sixty acres of land, if not already received. Soldiers of the late war are not entitled.

Land warrants purchased for cash at the highest market rates, and assignments perfected.

Correspondence invited.

Lemon sought to maintain a high-volume, full-service claim house. (*National Tribune*, March 22, 1883)

Table 5–2 *Selected claim-houses' share of business from racial and ethnic groups (based on first-pension applications among CPE sample members)*

Firm Owner	Percent of Clients Who Were			
	African Americans	Germans	Irish	Other Immigrants
George E. Lemon	3.7	4.3	4.0	6.8
Milo B. Stevens	4.5	5.2	3.4	9.1
Nathan W. Fitzgerald	4.3	3.9	3.0	5.8
William H. Lusk	3.3	17.6	46.9	5.9
Augustus P. Lloyd	49.6	1.9	3.9	5.8
Nathan Bickford	20.8	22.8	3.0	10.7

There are contrasting ways to interpret claim houses' tactics and their relationship with clients. On the one hand, critics from the nineteenth century to our own time have pointed to claim houses' predatory practices, particularly those that targeted black veterans. A War Department report, for example, declared that "the colored pensioners of the United States, more than any other class of claimants, are peculiarly the prey of the claim agents," and a study of Lloyd's firm concludes that black veterans in the Baltimore area were "easy targets for Baltimore's attorneys."[11]

"IMPORTANT TO COLORED SOLDIERS and their Heirs -- All soldiers or their heirs who have received $100 bounty, are entitled to from $100 to [$800] more, depending on dates of enlistment. Pensions for those wounded or disabled while in service. Widows and children are entitled to pensions. I have a record of all deceased colored soldiers showing their company, regiment and place of death, which I will furnish to anyone for [$2.50] for each name if on my list. I will obtain duplicates of lost discharges. Charge of desertion removed. I make colored claims a specialty. Particular attention paid to OLD and REJECTED claims. JOHN C. BENDER, 60[4] Edmond Street, [St.] Joseph, Mo."

This advertisement, by Missouri claim agent John C. Bender in an African-American newspaper, declares that "I make colored claims a specialty." (Reproduced by permission from *Christian Recorder*, July 10, 1884)

Other observers, however, insisted that *all* pension seekers were easy marks for claim agents. One agent asserted that "claimants for pensions belong, for the most part, to the uneducated class; and if they cannot employ a competent attorney, they employ somebody else"; a pension commissioner declared that the typical pension seeker was "poor, ignorant, and friendless, an easy prey to fears aroused by skillful threat or persuasions"; and a politician asserted that "the average veteran, while he may know all about his disabilities, is as ignorant as a babe of that great and complex fabric of legislation called the pension laws." Evaluating these contentions requires a shift in focus to the behavior of pension applicants.[12]

Table 5–3 shows rates of claim-house use among various groups of CPE sample members who submitted a new pension application. All groups made heavy use of the houses, with patronage steadily rising to 90 percent or more by the time of the disability law. Use by former slaves ran ahead of other groups, hinting at a vulnerability to claim-houses' tactics, but other explanations such as differing disabilities must also be considered.

Table 5–4 shows the results of a logistic regression of claim-house use on several factors that might have motivated pension seekers. An especially strong (or weak) claim might encourage applicants to forego or to seek assistance; the analysis equates strong claims with a war wound, and, following the discussion in previous chapters, identifies especially tenuous claims as those that included a mental illness. To control for the overall trend toward more claim-house use, the analysis also employs control variables for the arrears-law and disability-law periods. Each of the dummy variables for ethnic and racial groups compares the group's odds of using a claim house to those of native-born white veterans.

The table shows that, of the groups analyzed, only former slaves stand out: with other characteristics held constant, they were considerably more likely than native whites

Table 5-3 First-time pension applicants' use of claim houses, by period and racial/ethnic group, CPE sample members

Period	Percent of First-Time Applicants Using a Claim House					
	Native Whites	Germans	Irish	Other Immigrants	Former Slaves	Freeborn African Americans
Early general law (1862–79)	77.0	75.7	73.1	77.7	84.8	77.8
Arrears law (1879–90)	85.5	83.4	84.4	86.6	90.2	79.2
Disability law (1890–1907)	87.7	89.1	91.2	89.5	96.9	93.9

Table 5–4 *Comparative odds of claim-house use among first-time pension seekers, CPE sample members*

Variable	Mean	Odds Ratio
German born	.060	.972
Irish born	.051	.989
Other immigrant	.075	1.116
Former slave	.046	**2.505**
Freeborn African American	.011	1.103
Claim included war wound	.172	**.808**
Claim included mental illness	.043	**1.641**
Application in arrears-law period (1879–90)	.393	**1.621**
Application in disability-law period (1890–1907)	.368	**2.090**
Weighted number of cases	18,741	

Note: Odds ratios in boldface indicate $p < .05$

to use a claim house. Insofar as slave birth is a proxy for poverty and lack of education, this finding underscores ex-slaves' role as easy prey. Other variables' effects, however, belie a one-dimensional explanation. Natives, immigrants, and African Americans alike apparently estimated the credibility of their claim – veterans with a war wound were less likely to employ a claim house, while those with a mental illness were more interested in assistance.[13]

Thus, there is some truth in both perspectives on claim-house use. Though it exaggerates, the assertion that "not one veteran in a thousand could prepare his own case so that it would meet the requirements of the Pension Bureau" identifies a driving force behind the high rates of claim-house use by all veterans. The "easy prey" conclusion is likewise accurate insofar as it reflects the special needs of freedmen lacking the skills and resources to confront the pension bureaucracy.[14]

However, both perspectives ignore other realities of the claim-house enterprise. Pension-law complexity can hardly account for the steadily rising use of claim houses over time. The disability law was less complicated than the general law, and should have curbed the increase in claim-house employment after 1890; increasingly aggressive marketing probably explains the rising resort to claim agents.

Nor does contemporary commentary account for veterans' informed choices regarding claim-house assistance. A population of dupes would not have produced the odds ratios shown in Table 5–4: pension seekers, including ex-slaves, were capable of gauging their chances for success and acting accordingly.

Pension attorneys and claim houses played a complex role in the Union army pension system. At less contentious moments, the Pension Bureau could admit that "attorneys who are familiar with the pension laws, rulings, and decisions are a valuable aid to claimants by presenting their cases in an intelligent and painstaking manner," and Chapters 3 and 4 showed Bureau reviewers' positive response to agents' compliance with the rules. Yet there is no denying the corruption that unscrupulous claim agents introduced into the pension system. Given the variety of their unethical tactics, the approximately one hundred claim agents whom the government disqualified each year for "improper, illegal, and unprofessional conduct" constituted the tip of a very large iceberg.[15]

The misdeeds of Nathan W. Fitzgerald, owner of the second-largest claim house, illustrate the multiplicity of claim agents' devious practices. Fitzgerald was suspended by the Pension Bureau for filing fraudulent pension claims (including ones from ex-Confederate soldiers), abandoning other claims, misleading applicants about the law and their cases, and overcharging clients. In one instance, Fitzgerald threatened nonpaying clients with termination of their pensions, and in other cases he demanded a delivery fee for application forms that were meant to be free of charge. Fitzgerald was reinstated just before selling his business to George E. Lemon in 1884.[16]

There is also no denying that claim agents' practices took a heavy toll on impoverished veterans, especially African Americans. A member of Congress declared in 1870 that "of all the money due the colored pensioners in the entire South and paid by the Government, the pensioners get not more than one half, the balance being stolen from them by these harpies [i.e., claim agents]," and the swindling continued long afterward. In the 1890s, a claim agent in Virginia, having obtained pensions for "confiding colored claimants, many of whom could not count money," helpfully cashed the recipients' checks, deducting sums ranging from $15 to $2,000 (the latter in arrears cases).[17]

But a single focus on claim agents' machinations produces a misleading picture of predators and prey. If the increasingly widespread use of claim houses, and the heavy reliance on them by ex-slaves, were triumphs of marketing, variation in claim-house use based on the nature of veterans' claims was a hallmark of discerning customers. It is true that claim agents manipulated applicants and the pension system, but it is also clear that veterans, including those whose race and ethnicity should have made them "easy prey," frequently made decisions based on claim houses' potential usefulness. If the application-assistance enterprise was not the unfettered market that some hoped for, neither was it quite the case of fishing in a barrel that critics denounced.

6

Havens of Last Resort

T he experience of CPE sample members with the Union army pension system reveals much about the nature of disability, the intrigues of late-nineteenth-century policy administration, and the evolution of Gilded-Age culture. Official evaluation of veterans' disability claims varied by the color of their skin and their country of origin; the Pension Bureau and its physician-contractors engaged in a ceaseless tug of war over applicants' character and the meaning of disability; and late-nineteenth-century nativists achieved some success in branding certain immigrants as members of separate races.

But some veterans' experience with government benefits extended beyond the pension system. Congress, moved by accounts of ex-soldiers' suffering (and by the political potential of the "soldier vote"), authorized in 1865 an asylum for Civil War veterans whose disability and poverty required institutional care. By the century's end, the institution had expanded into a network of eight "homes" that had provided shelter and assisted living for 100,000 veterans. The system continued to grow, reaching a one-year peak of more than 35,000 residents in 1908.[1]

The formal purpose of the federal soldiers' homes roughly paralleled that of the pension system. Originally restricted to veterans whose service-related disabilities prevented them from earning a living, the homes were made available in the mid-1880s to ex-soldiers with any disabling condition. When they were admitted by the managers and agreed to military-style rules and discipline, residents had access to medical care, activities and entertainment, and park-like grounds. Indeed, the homes served as tourist attractions, drawing thousands of visitors each year and providing tangible evidence of governmental solicitude for soldiers' self-sacrifice.[2]

Race and ethnicity played a part in the character of these homes. On the one hand, the homes opened their doors to African-American veterans, allowing officials to declare that the races were "living together on friendly terms, without compulsion, or without thought of each other except as soldiers disabled in the cause of a common country." On the other hand, comparatively few black veterans took up residence in the homes. Despite black soldiers having been more than 8 percent of the Union army, African Americans typically made

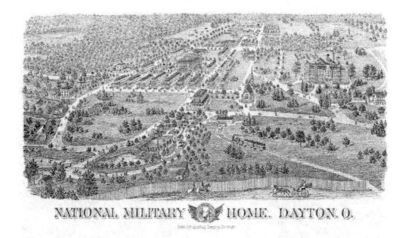

This logo of the Dayton, Ohio, federal soldiers' home shows its pastoral layout (ca. 1870). (Dayton VA Medical Center)

View of the buildings at the federal soldiers' home at Johnson City, Tennessee, opened in 1903. (Dayton VA Medical Center)

Tourists enjoy the grounds near the lakes at the Dayton soldiers' home. (Dayton VA Medical Center)

up less than 3 percent of soldiers' home residents, and only 104 black men enlisted in the CPE samples, approximately 3 percent of all black sample members who survived the Civil War, ever reported an address at a soldiers' home. Moreover, black residents slept in segregated quarters at the homes and ate separately from their white comrades.[3]

Veterans in the dining hall of the federal home in Marion, Indiana, in the late 1890s. (National Archives)

In contrast, foreign-born veterans populated soldiers' homes in numbers considerably above their wartime proportions, especially in the system's early decades. When politicians and home administrators felt obliged to account for this phenomenon, they focused on immigrants' rootlessness: one manager insisted that without the "relatives or special acquaintances in this country to whom they can apply when overtaken by sickness or distress," immigrants inevitably turned to soldiers' homes, whose shelter "they so well deserved."[4]

Interpreted with care, the CPE samples shed light on the inclination of African Americans and immigrants to seek or avoid soldiers' homes. Because identification of soldiers' home residents stems primarily from pension records, any analysis applies mainly to veterans who sought a pension. This identification method also means that dates indicating residence are "as-of" dates, rather than the actual date of entry into a home. This distinction is most evident in 1890–91, when the surge of new disability-law pension applicants included men who had earlier entered a soldiers' home; the analysis of residents in Table 6–3 includes a control for this anomaly. With these cautions, the CPE data offer insights into the decision to seek institutional living.[5]

Table 6–1 displays soldiers' home residence rates, that is, the number of veterans reporting a soldiers' home address per thousand person-years after the close of the Civil War. One striking pattern is the extraordinary degree to which Irish-born veterans found refuge in soldiers' homes: Irish Americans far exceeded all other groups in soldiers' homes until well into the twentieth century, reaching a maximum of 132 entrants per thousand veteran-years after eligibility was changed to include all forms of disability in the mid-1880s. Other immigrants, though they did not keep pace with the Irish, were also considerably more likely than native-born whites to reside in soldiers' homes in the nineteenth century. Indeed, the veterans least likely to resort to the homes were the native-born groups – African Americans and whites. These veterans disproportionately stayed away

Table 6-1 Soldiers' home residents per 1,000 person-years, CPE sample members

Period	U.S.-Born Whites	German Immigrants	Irish Immigrants	Other Immigrants	African Americans
1865–74	1.5	6.7	15.7	7.5	1.0
1875–84	4.5	13.4	33.1	13.1	.5
1885–94	18.2	48.3	132.5	47.3	9.2
1895–1904	27.2	46.3	83.2	48.1	24.7
1905–14	48.7	64.2	99.8	71.0	60.1
1915–24	54.4	60.8	49.7	72.4	39.6
Number of residents	1,156	140	340	193	104

Table 6-2 *Selected characteristics of soldiers' home residents before and after 1900, CPE sample members*

Characteristic	Before 1900	1900 or Later
Average age at report of residence	53.3	69.7
Percent hospitalized for wound during War	44.9	35.5
Percent never married	55.3	21.0
Number of entrants	857	1,030

from soldiers' homes until the turn of the century, when both groups' entry rates rose sharply. Black veterans' avoidance of the homes must thus be considered in light of changes over time.[6]

Table 6–2 shows other changes in the soldiers' home population. After 1900, the homes' transition from providing care for severely disabled veterans to housing the elderly becomes clear: new entrants were predictably older, and they were less likely to have suffered a war wound or been single before institutionalization. Changes over time also inform Table 6–3, which compares age, war wounds, race, and other factors in veterans' decision to seek out a soldiers' home.

Because singlehood is not the only indicator of the lack of "relatives or special acquaintances," the table uses an index of "rootlessness." This index is a "time-varying" estimate of available sources of care giving, beginning with a value of one for unmarried veterans; as the analysis underlying

Table 6–3 follows them year by year, the index is decreased by one when they married and increased when they were widowed, divorced, or separated, or when they took up residence in another state, any of which could deprive them of helping hands. It must be emphasized, of course, that this index is only a rough approximation of the permutations of living and caregiving arrangements possible among nineteenth- and early-twentieth-century Americans.[7]

Another time-dependent variable tracks CPE sample members' pension income. On the one hand, pensions provided an economic cushion that could enable ex-soldiers to avoid institutionalization; on the other hand, the connection of greater monthly payments to more serious disabilities signifies conditions that might require assisted living. As the observation of each veteran proceeds, he is credited with the monthly amount of his first pension and subsequent changes in payments as they occurred. The magnitude of the variable's hazard ratio suggests the primacy of pensions' economic or disability implications.

The table employs an additional variable for noncommissioned rank, because men accustomed to leadership could have balked at becoming a "private" in a soldiers' home. To allow for changes in the institutional population over the long history of soldiers' homes, Table 6–3 splits its analysis into the years preceding and following 1900; to allow for the apparent surge in residents resulting from new disability-law applicants, the pre-1900 analysis includes a control variable identifying veterans who exited from observation in

1890–91. The table includes the familiar columns showing means and hazard ratios, but it also reports a value for chi-square. This statistic allows direct comparison of variables' influence on soldiers' home residence, neutralizing the effect of differing units of measurement.

In the nineteenth century, older men and those with wounds were especially likely to seek institutional care, while former sergeants and corporals did indeed shy away from the homes. The economic value of pensions outweighed the disabilities they represented – the higher the monthly pension, the less likely an ex-soldier was to seek out a soldiers' home.

Race and ethnicity also affected veterans' decisions. The statistics for African Americans and immigrants compare each group to native-born whites: immigrants, especially the Irish, were more likely to take up residence in a soldiers' home, while black veterans, other characteristics being equal, were less likely to choose institutionalization.

After 1900, the toll of aging and the availability of pensions became widespread, causing age, noncommissioned rank, and pension income to fade as predictors of institutionalization. African-American veterans were now as likely as native-born whites to seek assisted living, but immigrants, again led by the Irish, remained somewhat more willing to turn to soldiers' homes. Because the latter tendency operated regardless of other characteristics, group character presents an appealing explanation: perhaps the Irish propensity for involvement in political, religious, and charitable institutions extended to soldiers' homes.[8]

Table 6–3 *Comparative likelihood of residence at a soldiers' home, CPE sample members*

Variable	Before 1900			1900 or Later		
	Mean	*Hazard Ratio*	*χ^2*	*Mean*	*Hazard Ratio*	*χ^2*
Year of birth	1838	**.956**	**99.9**	1840	1.005	.6
Wounded	.309	**1.667**	**50.5**	.312	**1.222**	**8.1**
Noncommissioned officer	.208	**.767**	**8.1**	.214	.883	2.1
Rootlessness index	.606	**2.179**	**295.1**	.865	**1.961**	**235.4**
Monthly pension income	$3.80	**.979**	**17.6**	$19.00	1.000	.1
African American	.066	**.221**	**20.0**	.057	1.152	.3
German born	.060	**2.371**	**53.7**	.052	**1.364**	**4.1**
Irish born	.049	**4.913**	**270.9**	.031	**2.167**	**23.2**
Other immigrant	.074	**2.057**	**44.3**	.069	**1.397**	**8.0**
Control variable: 1890–91	.020	**4.966**	**140.0**			
Weighted number of cases		20,126			12,953	

Note: Hazard ratios and chi-squares in boldface indicate p < .05

The CPE data can do little to test this suggestion, but Table 6–3 puts group motivations in perspective. The chi-square statistics indicate that any tendencies of the Irish to seek out soldiers' homes (and of African Americans to avoid them) were consistently overshadowed by individual circumstances. Veterans' decisions on institutionalization came first and foremost from the availability of caregivers. Losing a spouse, or losing kin and neighbors in a long-distance move, doubled the chances that a veteran would seek out a soldiers' home; marrying, which reduced the rootlessness index, halved his odds of institutionalization. Measured by chi-square, the influence of these characteristics outweighed the effect of Irish birth prior to 1900, and thereafter far exceeded the impact of race and ethnicity on decisions to enter or avoid a soldiers' home.

As much as commentators and pension administrators tried to elevate race and ethnicity into decisive factors, veterans' own behavior thus points to a different set of shared priorities. As physically attractive as soldiers' homes were, needy veterans' apparent first choice, whatever their race and ethnic background, was to turn to familiar caregivers. Native-born whites, immigrants, and African Americans reacted somewhat differently when caregivers were missing, but the consistently potent motivator of living choices was availability of "relatives or special acquaintances."[9]

Race and ethnicity may have affected veterans' institutionalization in other ways that the CPE data cannot reveal. Because prospective residents were required to establish occupational disability (and, before 1884, a service-related disability origin) to the satisfaction of soldiers' home managers, racial and ethnic patterns could lie behind managers' acceptances and rejections. Though investigation of managers' decision making is beyond the scope of this study, residence rates shown in Table 6–1 provide little reason to suspect widespread discrimination. Biased admission to soldiers' homes would likely have favored native-born white applicants, yet their institutionalization rates lagged far behind those of foreign-born veterans and were no higher than those of black veterans after 1900. These rates suggest that managers made good on the claim that their policies were inclusive. Officials of the Dayton, Ohio, branch, for example, declared that "any worthy soldier who has received an honorable discharge from the Army, if suffering under such a degree of disability that the privileges and comforts of such a home as this would be convenient to him, may enter the asylum," and the national managers insisted that "no soldier entitled to ask the benefits of the home has ever been denied shelter therein for any cause save his own ... misconduct."[10]

Application fraud did worry the homes' management, as in the case of one resident who was found to have gained admission by defrauding both the managers and the Pension Bureau. Evaluating a comparatively small number of men for a surrogate home, however, where they could be observed for first-hand evidence of good or ill behavior, apparently evoked a sympathetic official response. On the other hand, the task of evaluating a vastly larger number of men for a surrogate income, under relentless public criticism of "the dishonorable scramble for pensions," evidently persuaded the Pension Bureau to be unsparing in its judgment of applicants' character. A key lesson of this study is that as the stakes of decision making rose from the relatively low-key soldiers' home admission decisions to physicians' pension recommendations to the intensely scrutinized awarding of pensions, so did the reliance on racial and ethnic prejudice in reaching judgments.[11]

This lesson should in turn encourage reevaluation of the Pension Bureau. The Bureau has been deemed typical of the unformed condition of the Gilded-Age bureaucracy: the Bureau's impotence has been inferred from the small number of applications it rejected for fraud and its failure to persuade Congress to reform the medical-examination system.[12]

Yet the Pension Bureau's efficacy was more complex than these circumstances indicate. The pension commissioner did lose his struggle to replace the contractual system of local medical examiners with full-time physician-employees, and continuation of the much-maligned contract system hindered consolidation of the Bureau's power. It must also be noted, however, that commissioners felt no qualms about repeatedly asking Congress to change other features of pension legislation, with occasional success. Moreover, Congress's adoption of the Bureau's practice of investigating applicants' "vicious habits" was a grant of wide discretionary power to the Bureau and its evaluators.[13]

It is likewise true that the Pension Bureau rejected (and occasionally prosecuted) only a small proportion of applicants for outright fraud. Chapters 3 and 4 showed, however, that the Bureau freely exercised its discretionary power in rejecting one-fourth or more of pension seekers for failure to prove claims to reviewers' satisfaction.

The Bureau's exercise of discretion, as we have seen, also extended to apparent rejection of applicants based on race and ethnicity. This finding echoes a lesson conveyed by recent studies of bureaucratic development. As bureaucracies acquired latitude in the late nineteenth and early twentieth centuries, their purposes were not always ones we would applaud: they might include the Post Office's obsessive suppression of "vice" or, in the present case, denial of government benefits out of racial and ethnic prejudice.[14]

7

Epilogue

A challenge all authors face is anticipating incisive questions. We have tried to do so in the preceding chapters, and we now foresee an overarching query. We have found evidence of discrimination in benefits for Union army veterans with disabilities, consistent with ingrained prejudice against African Americans and rising hostility toward non-"Anglo-Saxon" immigrants. Seeing these results, a skeptic may ask, "You've found discrimination in a 150-year government benefits program. What's new, and what's changed?" We have four answers to these questions.

First, our purpose goes well beyond uncovering discriminatory treatment in a public program. We have also attempted to portray veterans' benefits in human terms, and to understand how prejudiced treatment occurred. A tale of three veterans provides an overview of our purpose and findings.

All three men were born in the mid-1840s. Hiram E. Smith served three years in the 8th Infantry of his native Connecticut, spending about half the time behind the lines as a nurse and carrying out other duties. David J. Thompson, born a slave in Virginia, joined the U.S. Colored Troops in the summer of 1864 and suffered a serious wrist wound at the siege of Petersburg. Samuel Guttmann, an immigrant from Poland, left his grocery store to join the 52nd New York Infantry in the same summer, serving through the War's end without serious harm.[1]

The three veterans submitted their first pension applications (with claim-house assistance) under the disability law, Guttmann applying in 1891 and Smith and Thompson the following year. Within a few months, the Pension Bureau verified military service and scheduled the men for a medical examination. Their disability claims were similar – all included kidney disease, heart trouble, and rheumatism. They encountered varied treatment from examining physicians: the surgeons recommended Smith for a pension for heart disease and rheumatism, while endorsing Thompson and Guttmann only for rheumatism.[2]

The Pension Bureau drew a considerably sharper distinction among these applicants. The Bureau awarded Smith, the native-born white veteran, a pension of $6 per month, but overruled the physicians' recommendations for Thompson and Guttmann and rejected their applications.

Three cases do not establish a pattern, but they illuminate the multivariate analyses of Chapters 3 and 4, which showed race (and ethnicity, after some immigrants were consigned to "races") playing an especially large role in Pension Bureau decisions. Racial and ethnic discrimination should not be viewed as a monolithic force: biased actions on pensions were much more common in the distant bureaucratic adjudication than in the face-to-face encounter.

Our second point is that the presumption of seamless prejudice cannot explain the key features of Tables 3–7 and 4–9. Not only did discrimination operate differently from level to level in the pension system; there were times when it did not consistently operate at all. Table 3–7 shows that black applicants fared better than whites until the application caseload became overwhelming, and Table 4–9 shows that foreign-born pension seekers were treated equitably until the late nineteenth century's nativist campaigns. Prejudice may be, as some would have it, "systemic" in American life, but we have found little evidence of uniformly prejudiced *actions*. The biases we reveal had contours shaped by time and circumstance: discrimination was a blunt instrument near to hand, but there were periods when it was left alone.[3]

Third, assumptions about prejudice and discrimination typically presume victimhood of those on the receiving end. In no way does it excuse discrimination to note that African Americans and foreign-born veterans refused to act like victims of the Union army pension system. For one thing, as benefits became more liberal and better publicized, African Americans and immigrants outpaced native whites in seeking access to the system. For another, rejected applicants seldom abandoned their efforts – David J. Thompson and Samuel Guttmann continued to submit applications until they received a pension.

Our sources also provide only scattered evidence that veterans felt doubly stigmatized by their race or ethnicity. Black veterans' occasional complaints must be seen in the larger context of their comrades' conceptions of masculinity: although some native whites characterized their disability as reduced manhood, no black applicants in the CPE samples did so. Moreover, we have seen that acknowledgment of a mental illness reduced a pension seeker's chances of success; as the foremost stigmatized disease, it should have been de-emphasized by African Americans and immigrants who wanted to avoid double stigmatization. Yet Tables 3–8 and 4–10 show that black veterans and immigrants included mental-illness claims approximately as often as did native whites.

Nor did race or ethnic background deter veterans from seeking shelter in a soldiers' home. The key influence on residence was lack of caregivers: in the immediate postbellum years, Irish-born veterans made disproportionate use of the soldiers' homes, but as veterans aged, race and ethnicity faded as important influences on residence. All of these results underscore relational concepts' ironic fullness and emptiness – race, embodied in African Americans and "inferior" immigrants, provided government officials a full explanation of character, but was frequently treated as a hollow reed by veterans themselves.

Our fourth point is that the interplay of social concepts, bureaucratic expediency, and individual initiative that shaped the Union army benefits system is vital to understanding the workings of more recent public policies. We noted in Chapter 2 that many of the rules for veterans' benefits were developed after previous wars, but the Civil War system was distinctive in facing unprecedented numbers of non-"white" veterans at a time of exceptional racial sensitivity. This confrontation led in directions explored in this book, directions which subsequent public policies eventually followed.

Disability compensation for veterans of the First World War, for example, was initially devised to avoid the vagaries of Civil War pensions. The earlier system's patchwork of payments was replaced by a comprehensive schedule of medical conditions, administered by staff physicians who would objectively determine claimants' service-related reduction in earning capacity and thus their compensation.[4]

Within a few years, however, this program acquired many of the Civil War system's features. Congress took it upon itself to earmark a condition (tuberculosis) for special compensation; the Veterans Bureau began to accept testimony from lay witnesses as well as from examining physicians (who were themselves supplemented by local contract physicians); and a racial bias appeared in administrative

judgments. Though the scale of discrimination in this program has not been quantified, the observed bias resembles
that of the Civil War system. Veterans Bureau administrators were known to overrule physicians' recommendations
for African Americans who were reportedly "not in need of
Government assistance," while black veterans themselves,
though they believed that "we are invariably received and
treated as a colored man and not as a disabled soldier," could
be persistent in asserting their rights.[5]

Prejudice likewise emerged in the extensive system of
benefits provided for veterans of the Second World War. In
1946, Congress provided for "re-rating" of disability payments, aimed at reducing compensation for veterans whose
condition had improved. The physicians assigned to these
re-evaluations, a combination of Veterans Administration
staff and outside contractors, conducted more than one
million examinations for benefits each year, and their attitude reveals racial prejudice. One physician declared that
African Americans' service "doesn't qualify them for royal-
ties from this man's Army," and a physician pointed to a
white veteran "and asked [a black ex-soldier] if I thought
that I should be getting more than the compensation that
he was getting." To a greater extent than their predeces-
sors, black veterans of the Second World War sought redress
through civil rights groups and veterans' organizations. For
example, one African American who had lost his disability
compensation wrote to the NAACP that "I have received an
awful injustice and demand that you adjudicate my claim,"

and other black veterans participated in public demonstrations for increased benefits.[6]

The decades following the Second World War witnessed a revolution in understanding of and responses to disability. Advocates for veterans and civilians with disabilities maintained a contentious relationship, but both groups, bolstered by the contemporary rights and protest movements, contributed to a wide-ranging de-emphasis of the medical model in favor of a rights-based approach to disability. As he signed the Americans with Disabilities Act in 1990, George H. W. Bush acknowledged the transformation: "Together we've begun to shift disability in America away from exclusion, towards inclusion; away from dependence, towards independence; away from paternalism, towards empowerment."[7]

In spite of these developments in disability and civil rights, recent evidence points to lingering discrimination in social services. One study has found that physicians continue to doubt black patients' self-discipline and intelligence, and another reveals that African Americans receive lower disability ratings and hence smaller awards for workers' compensation. And the Veterans Benefits Administration (VBA), the modern successor to the Pension Bureau, echoes many of the old bureaucracy's culture and attendant difficulties.[8]

The VBA, which administers compensation for service-related impairments and means-tested pensions for veterans with other disabilities, confronts a backlog rivaling that which plagued the Pension Bureau. As of this writing, the

VBA is more than 400,000 disability-rating cases behindhand, and the consequent problems are reminiscent of the Pension Bureau's troubles. Critics condemn the VBA's "emphasis of quantity over quality of work," which causes excessive attrition and "improper denials of benefits and inconsistent decisions." Such errors of harassed decision making, estimated at twenty to thirty percent of benefit cases, inevitably include racial bias: a recent study of VBA ratings finds that inspectors are considerably less likely to accept claims for post-traumatic stress disorder, for example, from African-American veterans.[9]

In linking these problems with our findings from more than a century ago, we ask the same question as do other comparative studies: what do differing contexts tell us about what we have found? The persistence of overwhelming caseloads and a racially prejudiced administration despite massive social changes points to discrimination's tenacity, and to our recommendations.

We found in Chapters 3 and 4 that racial discrimination lay dormant until the explosive growth of the Pension Bureau's workload. As long as attitudes toward disability remain tied to "worthiness," administrators must be unrelenting in their demand for the resources to conduct legitimate evaluations of benefit seekers.[10]

At the same time, our finding that ethnic discrimination emerged long after the onset of bias against African Americans suggests a more fundamental problem with veterans' disability benefits. Current law preserves the policy of character assessment by prohibiting pensions for disabilities resulting from "willful misconduct." The goal underlying this proscription is undoubtedly as laudable as was the Gilded Age's pursuit of "vicious habits"; we do not pretend to know a better way to achieve "justice, and justice alone." We suspect, however, that the survival of this calculus of character invites prejudicial short-cuts to adjudication. We urge a complete reconsideration of the premises, especially the burden of proof for credibility, on which veterans' disability benefits rest.[11]

We focused this investigation on a public policy's effects on the people who encountered it – the impact of ideas on the experiences of former Civil War soldiers with disabilities as they negotiated the system of military benefits. Whether black or white, or of Irish, Jewish, or other descent, today's generation of Americans with disabilities, including a growing number who are veterans, is the first to grow up with the civil and human rights set out in laws such as the Americans with Disabilities Act and the United Nations Convention on the Rights of Persons with Disabilities of 2008.

Will the stubborn ideas associated with disability – a medical model, and worthiness, capacity, and discrimination – persist, or will this generation continue to drive its experiences toward equal rights and inclusion? Answers to such questions will be informed by how we learn from our past.[12]

Appendix

The data that are this study's foundation come from several decades of investigation and collection by researchers under the leadership of Robert W. Fogel. Seeking information on nineteenth-century health, labor-force participation, and mortality, Fogel and his colleagues turned to an extraordinary source of longitudinal information, the Civil War military and pension records held by the National Archives. After surveying these records, the researchers designed a sample to comprise documents for the men who joined 331 military companies randomly drawn from the rosters of the Union army. The investigators and assistants began coding into data files all military service and hospital records for each enlisted man in these companies, added details from his pension file, and eventually included information for those recruits who could be located in U.S. census returns.[1]

At present, data collection is complete for the recruits in 303 companies of the original sample, recently supplemented by data from soldiers who served in fifty-two companies of the U.S. Colored Troops. Our investigation focuses on two differently organized data sets that contain the samples' information. The first, in which the unit of observation is the soldier, contains all of his extant military and pension information, from place of birth to cause of death, with the exception of the examining physicians' reports on his pension applications. Information from the latter reports appears in a separate file in which the unit of observation is the medical examination. In all, there are records for 35,570 white recruits and 6,155 African Americans in the military and pension files, and the results of 95,383 medical examinations for pension applicants in the surgeons' certificates files. The data sets, which we cite as the CPE samples, furnish the information on soldiers and veterans for our study.[2]

The samples contain an extraordinary wealth of detail on the life course of these men, but one modification has been necessary. The decision to apply for a pension, a key issue in Chapters 3 and 4, cannot be adequately assessed without considering each veteran's opportunity to apply – that is, how long he lived after the Civil War. Obtaining this information is rarely a problem for pension applicants: because evidence of a veteran's death began the process of dropping him from the pension rolls as well as procedures for obtaining a widow's or other dependent's pension, a death date is present for 93 percent of all CPE sample members who sought a pension. Nonapplicants, however, are much different: death dates, from widows' and dependents' applications and other documents, are available for only 15 percent of CPE sample members who did not apply for a pension. A bias of this magnitude against nonapplicants would ordinarily preclude analysis of the likelihood of applying for a pension.

Death dates that do exist for nonapplicants, however, reveal a striking pattern. Of nonapplicants with death dates, more than 80 percent died before 1890, whereas fewer than 5 percent of pension seekers were dead by then. To reflect this difference and to produce a more appropriate population at risk of applying, we have estimated years-to-live at mustering-out for "unknown" nonapplicants based on the years-to-live available for nonapplicants of the same age and race who do have death dates. For example, black nonapplicants who were discharged from the army at ages twenty to twenty-five had a life expectancy of 18.4 years, so a black nonapplicant with an unknown death date who was discharged in 1865 in his early twenties would be assigned an estimated death year of 1883.[3]

Because the central purpose of this adjustment is to incorporate the behavior of veterans who died without pension records before 1890, its main effect is to raise the number of nonapplicants in the general-law period. The adjustment adds 7,786 cases before 1890 and 486 afterward, and lowers the general-law application rate by 10.8 percentage points for whites and 8.9 points for African Americans, with smaller changes under the disability law.

Appendix

The wealth of information in the CPE samples calls for multivariate analysis of questions such as the influences on pension-approval decisions. Readers who find such techniques off-putting should reconsider them as tools that, viewed in their proper light, render assistance but do not replace logical inquiry.

The two multivariate methods employed in this study are logistic regression and hazards analysis. Both are rooted in the logic of sorting out predictor variables based on their association with an outcome. Logistic regression is based on the familiar concept of "odds": its results estimate the effect of each predictor variable, such as being African American, having been wounded, and so on, on the odds of being approved for a pension, for example, with every other predictor held constant. In this study's tables, these estimates are reported as "odds ratios" – if the odds of a white applicant being approved are set at 1.0, what is the effect of being an African American of the same age, location, and other characteristics? A ratio below 1.0 indicates lower odds, while a ratio above 1.0, say, 1.25, would mean a 25 percent increase in odds of approval associated with the variable in question. Odds ratios printed in boldface pass the conventional ".05 significance test" – that is, there is less than a 5 percent chance of their being a neutral 1.0 in the soldier population from which the CPE samples were drawn.

Logistic regression is appropriate for investigating the *results* of an event such as physicians' examination of a pension applicant, but how can we account for the *occurrence* of an event in the first place? This question's significance comes into focus when we consider issues of "risk" and specification of variables. The population to be analyzed for pension approval consists of those who applied, but what was the population at risk of applying, given that some veterans died in 1866 while others survived beyond the end of observation in 1907? Moreover, variables affecting application success include those such as residence at the time of application, but if we are interested in influences on seeking out a soldiers' home, how do we classify the marital status of a veteran who married in 1869 and was widowed in 1886? Hazards analysis is especially suited to the moving target presented by behavior followed over time.[4]

Hazards analysis rests on measurement of each soldier's time between his initial observation (enlistment or, for a veteran, his discharge) and either the event of interest (suffering a wound or disease, applying for a pension, or residing in a soldiers' home) or his exit from observation. This allows the procedure to compare, at each point in time, the characteristics of men who experienced the event of interest and those who did not. Having evaluated the "hazard" of pension application, for example, over the whole time covered, the procedure produces a hazard ratio for each independent variable, whose interpretation resembles that of the odds ratio.

To accommodate characteristics that changed over time, hazards analysis also allows for "time-varying" independent variables. In the problem of marital status posed above, the appropriate variable can be changed from single to married in the veteran's fourth year of observation, then from married to widowed in the twenty-first year, and the procedure evaluates the "risk" of soldiers' home residence accordingly.

Hazards analysis rests on the assumption that the effects of the independent variables on a risk remain stable over time. When the effects vary, typical remedies are to subdivide the time of observation into separate analyses, or to include a control variable that registers periods in which the relationship between predictors and events are plainly atypical. Several tables in this study employ one or both of these modifications.

Notes

Introduction

1. For uses of these "defects" as nouns denoting the people who had them, see Jeremy Bentham, "Situation and Relief of the Poor [1797]," in John Bowring, comp., *The Works of Jeremy Bentham* (Edinburgh: William Tait, 1843), 8: 362; *New General English Dictionary* (London: Topis and Bunney, 1781) (unpaged), entries under "blind" and "lunatick."

2. The paradigms are discussed in Peter Blanck, "'The Right to Live in the World': Disability Yesterday, Today, and Tomorrow–The 2008 Jacobus tenBroek Disability Law Symposium," *Texas Journal on Civil Liberties and Civil Rights* 13 (2008), 367–401; Peter Blanck, Eve Hill, Charles Siegal, and Michael Waterstone, eds., *Disability Civil Rights Law and Policy: Cases and Materials* (St. Paul, MN: Thomson/West, 2009); Catherine J. Kudlick, "Disability History: Why We Need Another 'Other,'" *American Historical Review* 108 (2003), 772–773; Paul K. Longmore and Lauri Umansky, eds., *The New Disability History: American Perspectives* (New York: New York University Press, 2001), 8–9; Susan Burch and Ian Sutherland, "Who's Not Yet Here? American Disability

History," *Radical History Review* 94 (2006), 128–129; Mary Crossley, "The Disability Kaleidoscope," *Notre Dame Law Review* 74 (1999), 649–660. The nineteenth-century rise of "normality" is asserted in Lennard J. Davis, *Enforcing Normalcy: Disability, Deafness, and the Body* (London: Verso, 1995), 24–25. The insight about disability equaling inability is from Kudlick, "Disability History," 769.

3. The pioneering study is Erving Goffman, *Stigma: Notes on the Management of Spoiled Identity* (Englewood Cliffs, NJ: Prentice-Hall, 1963). For a summary of recent studies, see Jo C. Phelan, Bruce G. Link, and John F. Dovidio, "Sigma and Prejudice: One Animal or Two?" *Social Science and Medicine* 67 (2008), 358–367. See also Rosemarie Garland-Thompson, *Staring: How We Look* (New York: Oxford University Press, 2009); Susan Schweik, *The Ugly Laws: Disability in Public* (New York: New York University Press, 2009).

4. *New York Times*, Sept. 16, 1882; Goffman, *Stigma*, 9–19, 43–48.

5. Frances Clarke, "'Honorable Scars': Northern Amputees and the Meaning of Civil War Injuries," in Paul A. Cimbala and Randall Miller, eds., *Union Soldiers and the Northern Home Front: Wartime Experiences, Postwar Adjustments* (New York: Fordham University Press, 2002), 386, 387. See also Laurann Figg and Jane Farrell-Beck, "Amputation in the Civil War: Physical and Social Dimensions," *Journal of the History of Medicine* 48 (1993), 454–475. Quotation on "melancholy" from Statement to Examining Board, Record of William Hackett (100th New York Infantry), March 1, 1884, *Surgeons' Certificates,* recruit's identification number 1310005081.

6. Clarke, "Honorable Scars," 371. See also Schweik, *Ugly Laws,* 184–204.

7. Studies of the creation of benefits for Civil War veterans include William H. Glasson, *Federal Military Pensions in the United States* (New York: Oxford University Press, 1918); Theda Skocpol, *Protecting Soldiers and Mothers: The Political Origins of Social Policy in the United States* (Cambridge, MA: Harvard University Press, 1992); Peter Blanck, "Civil War Pensions and Disability,"

Ohio State Law Journal 62 (2001), 117–122; John W. Oliver, "History of the Civil War Pensions, 1861–1885," *Bulletin of the University of Wisconsin*, History Series, 4 (1915), 1–120; Ann Shola Orloff, *The Politics of Pensions: A Comparative Analysis of Britain, Canada, and the United States, 1880–1940* (Madison: University of Wisconsin Press, 1993); Patrick J. Kelly, *Creating a National Home: Building the Veterans' Welfare State, 1860–1900* (Cambridge, MA: Harvard University Press, 1997). Race was largely absent from legislation regarding veterans, but laws and regulations governing benefits for veterans' survivors devoted significant attention to marriage and family connections among former slaves; see Elizabeth Ann Regosin, *Freedom's Promise: Ex–Slave Families and Citizenship in the Age of Emancipation* (Charlottesville: University Press of Virginia, 2002).

8. Though it tends to underestimate the efficacy of the Pension Bureau, Daniel P. Carpenter, *The Forging of Bureaucratic Autonomy: Reputations, Networks, and Policy Innovation in Executive Agencies, 1862–1928* (Princeton, NJ: Princeton University Press, 2001), provides an excellent analysis.

9. On the Bureau's complement, see *Report of Commissioner* [1904], 58th Cong., 3rd sess., 39, 42. Stenographers, copyists, and messengers are here counted as clerical; adding survivors to the number of ex-soldier employees would raise the veteran-preference proportion closer to 40 percent; see *Report of Commissioner* [1892], 52nd Cong., 2nd sess., 29.

10. See Regosin, *Freedom's Promise*; Beverly Schwartzberg, "'Lots of Them Did That': Desertion, Bigamy, and Marital Fluidity in Late-Nineteenth-Century America," *Journal of Social History* 37 (2004), 573–600; Megan J. McClintock, "Civil War Pensions and the Reconstruction of Union Families," *Journal of American History* 83 (1996), 456–480.

Chapter 1 The Winding Path of the Self and the Other

1. Mia Bay, *The White Image in the Black Mind: African-American Ideas about White People, 1830–1925* (New York: Oxford University

Press, 2000), 75–116; Joan Wallach Scott, "Gender as a Useful Category of Historical Analysis," *American Historical Review* 91 (1986), 1074. The literatures on race, ethnicity, and disability are vast, but some works are especially concerned with the mutability of these concepts. A sample of such works includes Winthrop D. Jordan, *White over Black: American Attitudes toward the Negro, 1550–1812* (Chapel Hill: University of North Carolina Press, 1968); George M. Fredrickson, *The Black Image in the White Mind: The Debate on Afro-American Character and Destiny, 1817–1914* (New York: Harper, Row, 1971); Audrey Medley, *Race in North America: Origin and Evolution of a Worldview* (Boulder, CO: Westview, 1993); Barbara Jeanne Fields, "Ideology and Race in American History," in J. Morgan Kousser and James M. McPherson, eds., *Region, Race, and Reconstruction: Essays in Honor of C. Vann Woodward* (New York: Oxford University Press, 1982), 143–177; Matthew Pratt Guterl, *The Color of Race in America, 1900–1940* (Cambridge, MA: Harvard University Press, 2001); Elliott West, "Reconstructing Race," *Western Historical Quarterly* 34 (2003), 7–26; Gail Bederman, *Manliness and Civilization: A Cultural History of Gender and Race in the United States, 1880–1917* (Chicago, IL: University of Chicago Press, 1995), 46–47; John Higham, *Strangers in the Land: Patterns in American Nativism, 1860–1925* (New Brunswick, NJ: Rutgers University Press, 1955), and idem, "Instead of a Sequel, or How I Lost My Subject," *Reviews in American History* 28 (2000), 327–339; David Roediger, *The Wages of Whiteness: Race and the Making of the American Working Class* (London: Verso, 1991); Matthew Frye Jacobson, *Whiteness of a Different Color: European Immigrants and the Alchemy of Race* (Cambridge, MA: Harvard University Press, 1998); Catherine J. Kudlick, "Disability History: Why We Need Another 'Other,'" *American Historical Review* 108 (2003), 763–793; the essays in Paul K. Longmore and Lauri Umansky, eds., *The New Disability History: American Perspectives* (New York: New York University Press, 2001); Susan Burch and Ian Sutherland, "Who's Not Yet Here? American Disability History," *Radical History Review* 94 (2006), 127–147; and the essays in David A.

Gerber, ed., *Disabled Veterans in History* (Ann Arbor: University of Michigan Press, 2000).

2. Quoted in Jacobson, *Whiteness of a Different Color*, 29, 30.

3. Frederick L. Hoffman, "The Race Traits and Tendencies of the American Negro," *Publications of the American Economic Association* 11 (1896), 242–243, 314, 327.

4. David J. Rothman, *The Discovery of the Asylum: Social Order and Disorder in the New Republic* (Boston: Little, Brown, 1971), 124; Douglas C. Baynton, *Forbidden Signs: American Culture and the Campaign against Sign Language* (Chicago, IL: University of Chicago Press, 1996), 49.

5. On causes and consequences of southerners' alarm, see Fredrickson, *Black Image*, 256–282; Edward L. Ayers, *The Promise of the New South: Life after Reconstruction* (New York: Oxford University Press, 1992), 132–159; Glenda Gilmore, *Gender and Jim Crow: Women and the Politics of White Supremacy in North Carolina, 1896–1920* (Chapel Hill: University of North Carolina Press, 1996); Bederman, *Manliness and Civilization*, 46–47. On subdivision of "whites," see Jacobson, *Whiteness of a Different Color*, 68–90.

6. Francis A. Walker, "Restriction of Immigration," *Atlantic Monthly*, June 1896, 828, 829. On developments leading to the Immigration Act of 1924, see Roger Daniels, *Coming to America: A History of Immigration and Ethnicity in American Life* (New York: HarperCollins, 1990), 270–284; Jacobson, *Whiteness of a Different Color*, 68–90.

7. Douglas C. Baynton, "Defectives in the Land: Disability and American Immigration Policy, 1882–1924," *Journal of American Ethnic History* 24 (2005), 31–44; see also Roxana Galusca, "From Fictive Ability to National Identity: Disability, Medical Inspection, and Public Health Regulations on Ellis Island," *Cultural Critique* 72 (2009), 137–163. The connection between "ugly laws" and immigration criteria is described in Susan M. Schweik, *The Ugly Laws: Disability in Public* (New York: New York University Press, 2009), 165–183.

8. William Wells Brown and Alexander Crummell, quoted in Bay, *White Image*, 93, 100. See also Bederman, *Manliness and Civilization*, 57–71.

9. *New York Times*, March 9, 1924; Paul K. Longmore and Paul Steven Miller, "'A Philosophy of Handicap': The Origins of Randolph Bourne's Radicalism," *Radical History Review* 94 (2006), 69, 72.

10. On Washington, see Ayers, *Promise of the New South*, 322–326. Bourne advised those with disabilities that they "must simply not expect too much"; Longmore and Miller, "Philosophy of Handicap," 69. On immigrants, see James R. Barrett and David R. Roediger, "The Irish and the 'Americanization' of the 'New Immigrants' in the Streets and in the Churches of the Urban United States, 1900–1930," *Journal of American Ethnic History* 24 (2005), 3–33; Robert M. Zecker, "'Negrov Lyncovanie' and the Unbearable Whiteness of Slovaks: The Immigrant Press Covers Race," *American Studies* 43 (2002), 43–72; Cynthia Skove Nevels, *Lynching to Belong: Claiming Whiteness through Racial Violence* (College Station: Texas A&M University Press, 2007).

11. "Manhood" and "manliness" are used here instead of "masculinity," following the rationale offered by Gail Bederman, who notes that "masculinity" meant simply biologically male through most of the nineteenth century, and was just gaining currency as connoting such traits as aggressiveness. See *Manliness and Civilization*, 17–20, 71–75.

12. *New York Times* quoted ibid., 36; Wells quoted ibid., 57.

13. Edward A. Ross, *The Old World in the New: The Significance of Past and Present Immigration to the American People* (New York: Century, 1914), 290, 294, 295. On Jewish efforts to refute stereotypes through sports, see, for example, Peter Levine, *Ellis Island to Ebbets Field: Sport and the American Jewish Experience* (New York: Oxford University Press, 1992), 144–169.

14. Sidney Webb and Beatrice Webb, *English Poor Law Policy* (London: Longman's, 1910), 8; John Williams-Searle, "Cold Comfort: Manhood, Brotherhood, and the Transformation of Disability, 1870–1900," in Longmore and Umansky, *New Disability History*, 157–186. See also Susan Burch, "Reading between the Signs: Defending Deaf Culture in Early Twentieth-Century America," in Longmore and Umansky, *New Disability*

History, 214–235. Wounded veterans were, however, occasionally exempted from the denigration of manhood implicit in local "ugly laws"; see Schweik, *Ugly Laws*, 149–150.

15. Quoted in Gary Kynoch, "Terrible Dilemmas: Black Enlistment in the Union Army during the American Civil War," *Slavery and Abolition* 18 (1997), 114, 123. See also Donald R. Shaffer, *After the Glory: The Struggles of Black Civil War Veterans* (Lawrence: University Press of Kansas, 2004), 119–142.

16. *SL,* 37th Cong., 2nd sess., 566–567; William H. Glasson, *Federal Military Pensions in the United States* (New York: Oxford University Press, 1918), 135.

17. *SL,* 2nd Cong., 2nd sess., 325; ibid., 39th Cong., 1st sess., 56; ibid., 51st Cong., 1st sess., 182.

18. On biennial examinations, see Glasson, *Military Pensions,* 75; *SL,* 35th Cong., 2nd sess., 489. Commissioner's statement in *Report of Commissioner* [1878], 45th Cong., 3rd sess., 822.

19. U.S. Pension Office, *Instructions to Examining Surgeons* (Washington, D.C.: Government Printing Office, 1873), 4; *SL,* 51st Cong., 1st sess., 182.

20. *Report of Commissioner* [1895], 54th Cong., 1st sess., 13.

21. *Report of Commissioner* [1894], 53rd Cong., 3rd sess., 14.

22. On the Union total of approximately 2.1 million soldiers (some estimates include sailors as well), see *Report of Commissioner* [1882], 47th Cong., 2nd sess., 723–725; U.S. Bureau of the Census, *Historical Statistics of the United States, Colonial Times to 1970* (Washington, D.C.: Government Printing Office, 1975), 2: 1140; James M. McPherson, *Battle Cry of Freedom: The Civil War Era* (New York: Oxford University Press, 1988), 306–307; Benjamin A. Gould, *Investigations in the Military and Anthropological Statistics of American Soldiers* (New York: Hurd and Houghton, 1869), 25. On the number of black soldiers, see *OR,* ser. 3, vol. 4, 1270; Gould, *Military and Anthropological Statistics,* 24. On the number of foreign-born soldiers, see ibid., 27.

23. Based on his interviews, the examiner recommended Schumacher for a pension. J. W. Abel to Pension Commissioner, Oct. 25, 1890, File of John Schumacher (80th Ohio Infantry), Pension Files.

Chapter 2 The Moral Economy of Veterans' Benefits

1. The number of ex-soldiers on the pension rolls reached 745,822 in 1898; William H. Glasson, *Federal Military Pensions in the United States* (New York: Oxford University Press, 1918), 271 (expenditure figures include pensions for widows and other dependents). For other overviews of the general-law system, see Theda Skocpol, *Protecting Soldiers and Mothers: The Political Origins of Social Policy in the United States* (Cambridge, MA: Harvard University Press, 1992), 103–107; Peter Blanck, "Civil War Pensions and Disability," *Ohio State Law Journal* 62 (2001), 117–122. On pension rates under the general law, see Glasson, *Military Pensions*, 133. On fractional ratings, see ibid., 136–138.

2. On pension attorneys and their activities, see Peter Blanck and Chen Song, "Civil War Pension Attorneys and Disability Politics," *Journal of Law Reform* 35 (2002), 137–217, and the discussion in Chapter 5 of the present study. On the arrears campaign, see Blanck, "Civil War Pensions," 122–123; Skocpol, *Protecting Soldiers*, 115–118. On pension expenditures, see *Report of Commissioner* [1891], 52nd Cong., 1st sess., 71.

3. On expenditures (including pensions for dependents), see Glasson, *Military Pensions*, 203. On age-related pensions, see *Report of Commissioner* [1898], 55th Cong., 3rd sess., 52; *Report of Commissioner* [1904], 58th Cong., 3rd sess., 28–32.

4. *New York Times*, May 5, 1893; William M. Sloane, "Pensions and Socialism," *Century*, June 1891, 183; *New York Times*, May 5, 1893, April 16, 1894.

5. See Glasson, *Military Pensions*, 54–97, 108–119; John P. Resch, *Suffering Soldiers: Revolutionary War Veterans, Moral Sentiment, and Political Culture in the Early Republic* (Amherst: University of Massachusetts Press, 1999).

6. Speech by Porter McCumber, *CR*, 59th Cong., 2nd sess., 806.

7. See Skocpol, *Protecting Soldiers*, 120–130; Glasson, *Military Pensions*, 204–238; Mary R. Dearing, *Veterans in Politics: The Story of the G.A.R.* (Baton Rouge: Louisiana State University Press, 1952); John W. Oliver, "History of the Civil War Pensions,

1861–1885," *Bulletin of the University of Wisconsin*, History Series, 4 (1915), 90–116. Some newspapers and magazines actively cooperated in the expansion campaign; see Blanck, "Civil War Pensions," 135–148.

8. In 1892, for example, the Pension Bureau reported receiving 2,000 congressional queries per day about unsettled claims; *Report of Commissioner* [1892], 52nd Cong., 2nd sess., 11, 16. On intervention and its results, see Charles J. Finocchiaro, "Constituent Service, Agency Decision Making, and Legislative Influence on the Bureaucracy in the Post Civil War Era," paper presented at History of Congress Conference, 2008.

9. Leonard D. White, *The Republican Era, 1869–1901: A Study in Administrative History* (Chicago: University of Chicago Press, 1958), 75–78; Glasson, *Military Pensions*, 280; Charles J. Finocchiaro, "Credit Claiming, Party Politics, and the Rise of Legislative Entrepreneurship in the Postbellum Congress," paper presented at annual meeting of American Political Science Association, 2007.

10. The sources for Figure 2–1 are the annual reports of the commissioner of pensions, beginning with the 1872–73 fiscal year's inauguration of consistent reporting and continuing until 1906–07, when service pensions were adopted. Many of the reports contain a convenient summary of applications *filed* and approvals, but filings are not the appropriate denominator for analysis of decision making, because of the large accumulation of unresolved applications; each report must thus be consulted for the yearly total of applications actually *evaluated*, which becomes the proper denominator. The ideal basis for the figure would be "original" applications, that is, applications by those who had never received a pension, but separate reporting of original claims ceased in 1892–93; Figure 2–1 thus reports decisions on all claims, including originals and other claims and claims by widows and other dependents as well as those from ex-soldiers. On the decline in approved claims in the 1870s, see *Report of Commissioner* [1874], 43rd Cong., 2nd sess., 656–657. On political influence in 1880, see U.S. House of Representatives,

Select Committee on Payment of Pensions, Bounty, and Back Pay, *Report on the Condition and Management of the Pension Bureau,* 46th Cong., 3rd sess., 388; *Report of Commissioner* [1885], 49th Cong., 1st sess., 111. On pension approvals in Cleveland's first administration, see Glasson, *Military Pensions,* 224; Larry M. Logue, "Union Veterans and Their Government: The Effects of Public Policies on Private Lives," *Journal of Interdisciplinary History* 22 (1992), 426–427.

11. James Tanner, quoted in Donald L. McMurry, "The Bureau of Pensions during the Administration of President Harrison," *Mississippi Valley Historical Review* 13 (1926), 348; Allen R. Foote, "Degradation by Pensions – The Protest of Loyal Volunteers," *Forum,* Dec. 1891, 427–428; *New York Times,* March 19, 1894.

12. See, for example, *New York Times,* April 28, May 26, May 29, July 2, July 11, 1893; Wiley Britton, *A Traveling Court: Based on the Investigation of War Claims* (Kansas City, MO: Smith-Grieves, 1926), 311. On the declining salience of pensions as a political issue, see Donald L. McMurry, "The Political Significance of the Pension Question, 1885–1897," *Mississippi Valley Historical Review* 9 (1922), 35–36.

13. Glasson, *Military Pensions,* 265, 266–269.

14. François Furstenberg, "Beyond Freedom and Slavery: Autonomy, Virtue, and Resistance in Early American Political Discourse," *Journal of American History* 89 (2003), 1295–1330. Furstenberg's argument is meant as an alternative to the "multiple traditions" view of American liberalism, especially as presented in Rogers M. Smith, *Civic Ideals: Conflicting Visions of Citizenship in U.S. History* (New Haven, CT: Yale University Press, 1997).

15. *New York Times,* April 16, 1894. On guidelines for ascertaining marriages, see *General Instructions to Special Examiners of the United States Pension Office* (Washington, D.C.: Government Printing Office, 1881), 24–25.

16. *Report of Commissioner* [1883], 48th Cong., 1st sess., 323–324; U.S. Pension Bureau, *A Treatise on the Practice of the Pension Bureau* (Washington, D.C.: Government Printing Office, 1898),

98–99. Well before the disability law of 1890, the Pension Bureau directed examining physicians to report "how far ... the habits of the applicant seem to affect his disability," and to note evidence of venereal diseases, but this was the limit of specificity on vicious habits. See U.S. Pension Bureau, *Instructions to Examining Surgeons* (Washington, D.C.: Government Printing Office, 1873), 6; *Instructions to Examining Surgeons* (Washington, D.C.: Government Printing Office, 1887), 12; after the disability law, *Instructions to Examining Surgeons* (Washington, D.C.: Government Printing Office, 1891), 6. In the transcribed details in *Surgeons' Certificates* (see Appendix for more details on this study's data), the physicians mentioned vicious habits (or their absence) in less than 1 percent of examinations. For similar findings, see Blanck, "Civil War Pensions," 166. In such cases the Pension Bureau called for "the testimony of two competent and credible witnesses, or of the family physician, ... to prove that the diseases alleged are not due to vicious habits"; *Treatise on the Practice*, 98.

17. *Report of Commissioner* [1884], 48th Cong., 2nd sess., 244; *Report of Commissioner* [1895], 54th Cong., 1st sess., 14; *Report of Commissioner* [1892], 52nd Cong., 2nd sess., 8; *Report of Commissioner* [1896], 54th Cong., 2nd sess., 8.

18. A. B. Casselman, "An Inside View of the Pension Bureau," *Century*, May 1893, 136; *Report of Commissioner* [1892], 9, 36; *New York Times*, Oct. 22, 1892. The 1891–92 fiscal year was actually a pre-1907 peak in approvals. For historians' evaluation of the Pension Bureau, see the mixed assessment in White, *Republican Era*, 208–221, and the decidedly negative judgment in Daniel P. Carpenter, *The Forging of Bureaucratic Autonomy: Reputations, Networks, and Policy Innovation in Executive Agencies, 1862–1928* (Princeton, NJ: Princeton University Press, 2001), 50, 59–60.

19. Carpenter, *Bureaucratic Autonomy*, 37–64; Adam McKeown, "Ritualization of Regulation: The Enforcement of Chinese Exclusion in the United States and China," *American Historical Review* 108 (2003), 377–403.

20. For details of the "sixty surgeon" proposal in a direct appeal to Congress (and endorsed by the Interior Department), see U.S. Senate, Committee on Pensions, Letter from Secretary of Interior to Committee on Pensions, 45th Cong., 2nd sess. On the proposal's fate, see Oliver, "Civil War Pensions," 46–47. See also Carpenter, *Bureaucratic Autonomy*, 59–60; Skocpol, *Protecting Soldiers*, 119–120.
21. McKeown, "Ritualization," 387.
22. Useful summaries of the application and evaluation process are in U.S. Department of Interior, *Annual Report* [1891], 52nd Cong., 1st sess., 70–73, and U.S. Pension Bureau, *A Treatise on the Practise of the Pension Bureau* (Washington, D.C.: Government Printing Office, 1898).
23. Donald R. Shaffer, *After the Glory: The Struggles of Black Civil War Veterans* (Lawrence: University Press of Kansas, 2004), 209, finds that 64 percent of sampled black veterans ever applied for a pension, compared to 77 percent of whites; Peter Blanck and Chen Song, "Civil War Pensions for Union Army Veterans: Race and Disability," paper presented at National Bureau of Economic Research Cohort Studies Meeting, 2004, finds that applications from black veterans were 9.2 percent of all pension applications, yet African Americans made up 14.5 percent of the soldiers analyzed.
24. Glasson, *Military Pensions*, 138. See also Peter Blanck and Michael Millender, "Before Disability Civil Rights: Civil War Pensions and the Politics of Disability in America," *Alabama Law Review* 52 (2000), 1–50.
25. Testimony of Joseph F. Atwood, in U.S. House, *Report on the Pension Bureau*, 138.

Chapter 3 African-American Veterans and the Pension System

1. *Report of Commissioner* [1870], 41st Cong., 3rd sess., 434; John W. Oliver, "History of the Civil War Pensions, 1861–1885," *Bulletin of the University of Wisconsin*, History Series, 4 (1915), 34; U.S. Pension Bureau, *General Instructions to Special Examiners of the U.S. Pension Office* (Washington, D.C.: Government Printing

Office, 1881), 24–25; Donald R. Shaffer, *After the Glory: The Struggles of Black Civil War Veterans* (Lawrence: University Press of Kansas, 2004), 130; E. B. French to Secretary of War, April 24, 1872, in U.S. Senate, Committee on Appropriations, *Estimates of Claims of Colored Soldiers and Sailors,* 45th Cong., 2nd sess., 12 (emphasis in original). See also Elizabeth Regosin, *Freedom's Promise: Ex-Slave Families and Citizenship in the Age of Emancipation* (Charlottesville: University Press of Virginia, 2002).

2. Affidavit of J. C. Carrick, n.d., affidavit of Clay Ballard, n.d., File of Clay Ballard (116th U.S. Colored Infantry), Pension Files.

3. J. F. Kinney to Secretary of Interior, Oct. 9, 1897; J. F. Raub to F. D. Stephenson, May 21, 1898; Percy S. Crowe to Commissioner of Pensions, Feb. 11, 1899, all ibid.

4. Deposition of F. O. Young, Feb. 9, 1899, ibid.

5. On the two costly battles, see William Glenn Robertson, "From the Crater to New Market Heights," in John David Smith, ed., *Black Soldiers in Blue: African American Troops in the Civil War Era* (Chapel Hill: University of North Carolina Press, 2002), 169–199; Peter Burchard, *One Gallant Rush: Robert Gould Shaw and His Brave Black Regiment* (New York: St. Martin's, 1965). Combat mortality figures are from *OR*, 3rd ser., 3: 667. On black soldiers' assignments, see John David Smith, "Let Us All Be Grateful That We Have Colored Troops That Will Fight," in idem, *Black Soldiers in Blue,* 42–43; Joseph T. Glatthaar, *Forged in Battle: The Civil War Alliance of Black Soldiers and White Officers* (New York: Free Press, 1990), 182–185.

6. Death rates are from *OR*, 3rd ser., 3: 669. On reasons for the difference, see Smith, "Let Us All Be Grateful," 41–42; Glatthaar, *Forged in Battle,* 187–195; Andrew K. Black, "In the Service of the United States: Comparative Mortality among African-American and White Troops in the Union Army," *Journal of Negro History* 79 (1994), 317–333.

7. Table 3–1 tabulates disease cases irrespective of severity; see Chapter 4, note 9 for a discussion of implications of "serious" maladies versus all diseases. Death rates for disease-sufferers in the CPE samples exclude those who were killed in combat or died of wounds.

8. The application rates reported here differ from those reported in Shaffer, *After the Glory*, 209 (see Chapter 2, note 23), because the latter study uses soldiers or their dependents who appear in Pension Bureau files as the denominator; the CPE rates reported here are based on all enlisted men in the samples.

9. The population "at risk" to apply for a pension after 1890, shown in the second row of Table 3–2, includes only those who were known (or estimated, according to the method described in the Appendix) to be alive and had not yet applied. The reduced denominators in Table 3–2 compared to Table 3–1 are due to veterans with discrepant discharge and first-application dates (the former should precede the latter), who are excluded.

10. Shaffer, *After the Glory*, 123–126.

11. Census comparisons are derived from the IPUMS samples (Steven Ruggles et al., *Integrated Public Use Microdata Series: Version 3.0* [machine-readable database] [Minneapolis: Minnesota Population Center, 2004]). Because county of birth was not recorded in the census and because Maryland was nearly evenly divided between slaves and free African Americans, Maryland is excluded from the figures for 1870. The comparable literacy figure for white men in 1870 is 91 percent. Property averages are based on census-listed real and personal property combined.

12. Age, which potentially influenced the likelihood of applying for a pension, is not included in Table 3–3 because it was used in estimating the survival of nonapplicants (see Appendix). Class, typically signified by occupation, is another factor that cannot be assessed in most of this study's analyses. Occupation was consistently recorded for new recruits and can reliably be used in the wartime analyses presented in Chapter 4; most other analyses, however, address behavior and circumstances decades after enlistment, rendering prewar employment largely irrelevant. Examining physicians began recording pension applicants' employment in the early twentieth century, and some of the CPE sample members have been linked to the federal censuses, but occupation is nonetheless unavailable for the majority of sample members.

13. See Dora L. Costa and Matthew E. Kahn, "Forging a New Identity: The Costs and Benefits of Diversity in Civil War Combat Units for Black Slaves and Freemen," *Journal of Economic History* 66 (2006), 936–962. The places that supplied the units with the most freemen were Maryland, Delaware, Virginia, and the District of Columbia.

14. If used alone instead of in conjunction with border-area enlistment, the percentage of freeborn company comrades produces a statistically significant effect (hazard ratio 1.007, meaning that a 50-percentage-point increase in freeborn comrades raised the likelihood of applying by 35 percent), but place of enlistment reduces the comrades' effect to the net shown in Part B of Table 3–3.

15. On a late-nineteenth-century "health crisis" among African Americans, see Kenneth F. Kiple and Virginia H. King, *Another Dimension to the Black Diaspora: Diet, Disease, and Racism* (New York: Cambridge University Press, 1981), 187–190; for a more polemical view, see W. Michael Byrd and Linda A. Clayton, *An American Health Dilemma: A Medical History of African Americans and the Problem of Race*, (New York: Routledge, 2000), 1: 325–357. See also Dora L. Costa, "Race and Older Age Mortality: Evidence from Union Army Veterans," National Bureau of Economic Research Working Paper 10902, 2004; Douglas Ewbank, "History of Black Mortality and Health before 1940," *Milbank Memorial Fund Quarterly* 65 supp. 1 (1987), 100–128; Samuel H. Preston and Michael R. Haines, *Fatal Years: Child Mortality in Late Nineteenth-Century America* (Princeton, N.J.: Princeton University Press, 1991), 81–85.

16. *Report of Commissioner* [1900], 56th Cong., 2nd sess., 47–48; Mary Frances Berry, *My Face Is Black Is True: Callie House and the Struggle for Ex-Slave Reparations* (New York: Knopf, 2005), 83, 33–74, 93–121.

17. Joseph Cannon, quoted ibid., 74; *New York Times*, June 20, 1893. See chapter 5 for additional analysis of claim-house use.

18. File of Willis Pleasant (119th U.S. Colored Infantry), Pension Files, passim. In the late 1890s the Pension Bureau ruled that

applicants 65 and older would generally be allowed the minimum pension, whereas those 75 and older would be assigned "senility" as a disability; see *Report of Commissioner* [1898], 55th Cong., 3rd sess., 52. A presidential order in 1904 authorized the Bureau to classify applicants 62 and older as one-half disabled and 70 and older as fully disabled (see Chapter 2); Willis Pleasant was born in 1830.

19. Physicians' reports taken from *Surgeons' Certificates*. The unit of observation in this file is the medical examination, whereas the unit of observation in *MPM Records* is the veteran, who might have a number of medical examinations in his file. Linking the first application to the first examination presents difficulties due to missing and out-of-order dates; see Richard W. Evans, "Integration of the Surgeon's Certificates with the Pension Application Groupings in the Union Army Dataset," Working Paper, Center for Population Economics, University of Chicago, 2003. Following Evans's suggestions, Tables 3–5 and 3–6, which require linking examinations in *Surgeons' Certificates* with Pension Bureau rulings in *MPM Records,* use only those examinations whose date follows a known first application date; Table 3–5, which uses *Surgeons' Certificates* alone and has the examination as the unit of analysis, uses the somewhat larger number of all first examinations for an "original" pension.

20. U.S. Pension Bureau, *Instructions to Examining Physicians* (Washington, D.C.: Government Printing Office, 1884), 9. There was a space for "complexion" on the physicians' report form in the 1870s, and physicians occasionally added a notation on skin color in later reports; see U.S. Pension Bureau, *Instructions to Examining Physicians* (Washington, D.C.: Government Printing Office, 1873), 3.

21. On mental illness in this period, see Eric T. Dean, Jr., *Shook over Hell: Post-Traumatic Stress, Vietnam, and the Civil War* (Cambridge, MA: Harvard University Press, 1997), 135–151; Charles E. Rosenberg, "Body and Mind in Nineteenth-Century Medicine: Some Clinical Origins of the Neurosis Construct," *Bulletin of the History of Medicine* 63 (1989), 185–197; Gerald

N. Grob, *The Mad among Us: A History of the Care of America's Mentally Ill* (New York: Free Press, 1994), 27–28, 55–77, 129–164. See also Erving Goffman, *Stigma: Notes on the Management of Spoiled Identity* (Englewood Cliffs, NJ: Prentice–Hall, 1963); Michael Waterstone and Michael Stein, "Disabling Prejudice," *Northwestern University Law Review* (forthcoming).

22. Black veterans are weighted downward to comprise 8.4 percent of total applicants in Tables 3–5 and 3–6 (see Appendix).

23. Overall examining-physician approval rates rose by 14.4 percentage points in the North and 10.9 in the South after 1890.

24. *Report of Commissioner* [1893], 53rd Cong., 2nd sess., 10–11; U.S. Pension Bureau, *Instructions to Examining Surgeons* (Washington, D.C.: Government Printing Office, 1893), 16; *Instructions to Examining Surgeons* (Washington, D.C.: Government Printing Office, 1895), 16–17. One of Cleveland's pension commissioners proposed "to detail experts from the medical division to visit and instruct the 1,285 boards throughout the country" regarding examinations and reporting; *Report of Commissioner* [1896], 54th Cong., 2nd sess., 12.

25. As noted in Chapter 2, examining physicians seldom mentioned the presence or absence of "vicious habits," but when they did there is no evident bias against black applicants: examiners reported no vicious habits in 29 percent of all mentions of white applicants' habits, and no vicious habits in 49 percent of reports on black applicants' habits; the number of mentions (123 for black applicants) is too small to divide meaningfully by skin color.

26. Testimony of Joseph F. Atwood, in U.S. House of Representatives, Select Committee on Payment of Pensions, Bounty, and Back Pay, *Report on the Condition and Management of the Pension Bureau*, 46th Cong., 3rd sess., 133.

27. *Report of Commissioner* [1875], 44th Cong., 1st sess., 440; *Report of Commissioner* [1884], 48th Cong., 1st sess., 247; *Report of Commissioner* [1892], 52nd Cong., 2nd sess., 37; *Report of Commissioner* [1898], 55th Cong., 3rd sess., 75.

28. By the 1890s, the medical division of the Pension Bureau employed a medical referee and his assistant, plus varying numbers of

medical reviewers; for a brief history of the division, see *Report of Commissioner* [1883], 48th Cong., 1st sess., 337–339. Most references to these officials in this study will use the collective term "reviewers."

29. The Pension Bureau sometimes overruled physicians in the other direction, awarding a pension when the physicians had found no pensionable disability; such actions were infrequent, however, occurring in only ten percent of first applications in the CPE samples.

30. *Report of Commissioner* [1872] 42nd Cong., 3rd sess., 335.

31. *Report of Commissioner* [1876], 44th Cong., 2nd sess., 704–705; Pension record of Thomas French (8th Connecticut Infantry), *MPM Records,* recruit's identification number 100805031. On evaluation of hernias in veterans and the condition's effects, see Chen Song and Louis L. Nguyen, "The Effect of Hernias on the Labor Force Participation of Union Army Veterans," in Dora L. Costa, ed., *Health and Labor Force Participation over the Life Cycle* (Chicago: University of Chicago Press, 2003), 253–310.

32. The medical division employed a referee, his assistant, and twenty examiners in 1882–83; *Report of Commissioner* [1883], 48th Cong., 1st sess., 339. The complement in 1891–92 was the referee and assistant, thirty-eight examiners, two surgeons, three principal examiners, and one special medical examiner; *Report of Commissioner* [1892], 52nd Cong., 2nd sess., 36.

33. The pension caseload is tabulated in the same manner as in Chapter 2. The slightly different rejection rate implied by Table 3–4 is largely due to Pension Bureau reversals of physicians' rejections, which are included in Table 3–4 but excluded from Table 3–7's reporting of rejections only.

34. *Report of Commissioner* [1870], 41st Cong., 3rd sess., 434.

35. Disease cases reported in U.S. Surgeon General's Office, *Medical and Surgical History of the Civil War* (Wilmington, NC: Broadfoot, 1990 [orig. pub. 1870]), 5: 636–637, 640–641, 710, 712. These cases, based on quarterly hospital reports filed during the War, are undercounted (see ibid., 5: 2–6), and should be taken as illustrating the order of magnitude of intestinal disorders versus

wounds. Table 3–8 begins with the disabilities that appear most frequently in the aggregate of all applications across races and periods; see also Blanck, "Civil War Pensions," 163. Percentages in each section's first column in Table 3–8 are the proportion of claims that mentioned each condition; since claims often included multiple disabilities, the percentages may sum down the column to more than 100. The percentages in the physicians column refer to the proportion of pension recommendations when applicants mentioned the disability, and the Pension Bureau column refers to the proportion of physician recommendations that the Bureau approved.

36. "Diarrhea" as used in this chapter also includes dysentery. Black soldiers suffered a reported 806 cases of these diseases per 1,000 soldier-years, compared to a rate of 563 per 1,000 white soldier-years; calculated from *Medical and Surgical History*, 1: 636–637, 710 (but see also the acknowledgment of undercounting discussed above).

37. Testimony of George M. Van Buren, in U.S. House, *Report on the Pension Bureau*, 163.

38. See Larry M. Logue and Peter Blanck, "'There Is Nothing That Promotes Longevity Like a Pension': Disability Policy and Mortality of Civil War Union Army Veterans," *Wake Forest Law Review* 39 (2004), 49–67; idem, "'Benefit of the Doubt': African American Civil War Veterans and Pensions," *Journal of Interdisciplinary History* 38 (2008), 394–397; Martin Salm, "The Effect of Pensions on Longevity: Evidence from Union Army Veterans," Discussion Paper No. 2668, Institute for the Study of Labor, Bonn, Germany, 2007.

39. Statements to Examining Board, Record of George Fauble (83rd Illinois Infantry), Oct. 31, 1891, recruit's identification number 2108309046; Record of James Toner (1st Delaware Infantry), Feb. 25, 1883, recruit's identification number 1100108167; Record of William Fetterly (41st Ohio Infantry), Dec. 11, 1895, recruit's identification number 2404109012; Record of Henry Rhodhamel (147th Ohio Infantry), Feb. 1899, recruit's identification number 2414701064; Record of Solomon Simpson (81st Indiana Infantry), July 19, 1893, recruit's identification number 2208107057; Record

of William Patterson (10th Michigan Infantry), Oct. 31, 1888, recruit's identification number 2301002075; Record of Alain Hank (2nd Michigan Infantry), Dec. 19, 1888, recruit's identification number 2300204041; Record of William Bullen (45th Wisconsin Infantry), June 19, 1889, recruit's identification number 2504501024; all in *Surgeons' Certificates.*

40. Statements to Examining Board, Record of Stephen Lee (116th Colored Infantry), Oct. 3, 1906, recruit's identification number 9011611160; Record of Jack Troupe (106th Colored Infantry), Feb. 25, 1885, recruit's identification number 9010603193; ibid.

41. Pension record of Levi H. Showell (9th U.S. Colored Infantry), *MPM Records,* recruit's identification number 9000903181.

Chapter 4   Pensions for Foreign-Born Veterans

1. For a sampling of recent studies of ethnic units, see Donald Allendorf, *Long Road to Liberty: The Odyssey of a German Regiment in the Yankee Army* (Kent, OH: Kent State University Press, 2006); Joseph G. Bilby, *Remember Fontenoy! The 69th New York and the Irish Brigade in the Civil War* (Hightstown, NJ: Longstreet House, 1995); Michael Bacarella, *Lincoln's Foreign Legion: The 39th New York Infantry, the Garibaldi Guard* (Shippensburg, PA: White Mane, 1996); James S. Pula, *The Sigel Regiment: A History of the 26th Wisconsin Volunteer Infantry, 1862–1865* (Campbell, CA: Savas, 1998). For studies that use the ethnic-unit approach as the basis for broader surveys of immigrant soldiers, see Ella Lonn, *Foreigners in the Union Army and Navy* (Baton Rouge: Louisiana State University Press, 1951); William L. Burton, *Melting Pot Soldiers: The Union's Ethnic Regiments* (Ames: Iowa State University Press, 1988); Dean B. Mahin, *The Blessed Place of Freedom: Europeans in Civil War America* (Washington, D.C.: Brassey's, 2002); David L. Valuska and Christian B. Keller, eds., *Damn Dutch: Pennsylvania Germans at Gettysburg* (Mechanicsburg, PA: Stackpole, 2004).

2. It must be noted that the ethnic character of military units fluctuated with the pace and composition of enlistments; the

percentages given here refer to the composition of companies at the War's end.

3. Biographies of foreign-born military men include Hans L. Trefousse, *Carl Schurz: A Biography* (New York: Fordham University Press, 1998); Roy Foster, John M. Hearne, and Rory T. Cornish, eds., *Thomas Francis Meagher: The Making of an Irish American* (Portland, OR: Irish Academic Press, 2005); Stephen D. Engle, *The Yankee Dutchman: The Life of Franz Sigel* (Fayetteville: University of Arkansas Press, 1993). A study that does address the experience of foreign-born veterans is Peter Blanck and Chen Song, "With Malice toward None, with Charity toward All: Civil War Pensions for Native and Foreign-Born Union Army Veterans," *Transnational Law and Contemporary Problems* 11 (2001), 1–75. See also Earl J. Hess, ed., *A German in the Yankee Fatherland: The Civil War Letters of Henry A. Kircher* (Kent, OH: Kent State University Press, 1983), 62; Susannah U. Bruce, *The Harp and the Eagle: Irish-American Volunteers and the Union Army, 1861–1865* (New York: New York University Press, 2006), 233–262.

4. Studies that include ethnicity as a factor in wartime casualties include Maris A. Vinovksis, "Have Social Historians Lost the Civil War? Some Preliminary Demographic Speculations," *Journal of American History* 76 (1989), 34–58; Daniel Scott Smith, "Seasoning, Disease Environment, and Conditions of Exposure: New York Union Army Regiments and Soldiers," in Dora L. Costa, ed., *Health and Labor Force Participation over the Life Cycle* (Chicago: University of Chicago Press, 2003), 89–112.

5. See especially Warren A. Craig, "'Oh, God, What a Pity!' The Irish Brigade at Fredericksburg and the Creation of Myth," *Civil War History* 47 (2001), 193–221; Susannah U. Bruce, "'Remember Your Country and Keep Up Its Credit': Irish Volunteers and the Union Army, 1861–1865," *Journal of Military History* 69 (2005), 331–359.

6. Col. Patrick Guiney, quoted in Mahin, *Blessed Place of Freedom*, 126; Christian B. Keller, "Pennsylvania and Virginia Germans during the Civil War: A Brief History and Comparative Analysis," *Virginia Magazine of History and Biography* 109 (2001), 37–86.

7. Bruce, "Remember Your Country," 358; Keller, "Pennsylvania and Virginia Germans," 58.

8. Warren, "What a Pity," 202; Mahin, *Blessed Place of Freedom*, 17.

9. The compilers of the CPE samples included a notation of battles for the member's company, gathered from regimental histories plus other notations in hospital and pension records. Battles identified in Table 4–2 are major engagements that included substantial participation by foreign-born troops; a description of these battles is included in Lonn, *Foreigners in the Union Army*. The noncommissioned-rank and battle variables are defined as time-varying – that is, a sample member was classified as a noncommissioned officer as of the month of his promotion, and he became "at risk" of participating in a battle if and when his time under observation passed the date of the battle (see also the discussion in the Appendix).

10. Quoted in Bell I. Wiley, *The Life of Billy Yank: The Common Soldier of the Union* (Indianapolis: Bobbs-Merrill, 1952), 300. A similar relationship between age and wounding was found among soldiers from Newburyport, Mass; Vinovskis, "Have Social Historians Lost," 49. There was an increase in wounds at the oldest ages, but the author notes that the Newburyport results do not control for time served; the hazards model used in Table 4–2 allows for the length of wartime service.

11. See generally John D. Billings, *Hardtack and Coffee* (Boston, MA: G. M. Smith, 1887), 4, 104–105, 205–207. On color bearers, see Wiley, *Billy Yank*, 93–94.

12. On German performance, see Stephen W. Sears, *Chancellorsville* (Boston, MA: Houghton Mifflin, 1996), 284–286, 432–433; Keller, "Pennsylvania and Virginia Germans." It should be noted that the small magnitude of the hazard ratio for company percent Irish is somewhat misleading: each 1-percent rise in Irish members raised the risk of being wounded by 1 percent. Another way of expressing this variable's importance is with chi-square (not shown in the table), which compares variables' effects irrespective of units of measurement. After the battle variables, the variable with the largest chi-square value is the company percent Irish.

13. Kircher to mother, Jan. 30, 1863, in Hess, *German in the Yankee Fatherland*, 62.

14. The CPE samples include army surgeons' comments about the severity of maladies they encountered. Because serious illnesses caused the most trauma during the War (and were most likely to elicit comments such as those by Henry Kircher), Tables 4–3 and 4–4 use diseases described by a physician as "severe," "acute," or "chronic"; since any illness could cause problems in later life, illness variables in tables (including those in Chapter 3) that address pension eligibility refer to any illness that led to hospitalization, irrespective of physician comments. For a reference to mid-nineteenth-century cities as "virtual charnel houses," see Michael R. Haines, "The Urban Mortality Transition in the United States, 1800 to 1940," *Annales de Démographie Historique* (2001), 37. See also Gerald N. Grob, *The Deadly Truth: A History of Disease in America* (Cambridge, MA: Harvard University Press, 2002), 96–120. "First service" denotes first regimental posting away from the area of recruitment; the importance of this variable is identified in Smith, "Seasoning." To avoid the potentially nebulous circumstance of wounds and disease coinciding or causing one another, soldiers who were wounded are followed in the analysis given in Table 4–4 until the wound and then removed from observation. Noncommissioned rank is analyzed in Table 4–4 as a time-dependent variable, with the higher rank applying in the month of promotion for those who enlisted as privates.

15. Burton, *Melting Pot Soldiers*, 148. Tents for noncommissioned staff were to be forty paces behind those of enlisted men, twenty paces in front of the company officers; see U.S. War Department, *Revised Regulations for the Army of the United States, 1861* (Philadelphia, PA: George W. Childs, 1862), 76–77.

16. *National Tribune*, Aug. 27, Sept. 24, 1891.

17. Asa W. Bartlett, *History of the Twelfth Regiment, New Hampshire Volunteers in the War of the Rebellion* (Concord., NH: Ira C. Evans, 1897), 153. Similar invective was directed at "bounty jumpers," enlistees who collected a bounty, deserted, and then enlisted again elsewhere after collecting another bounty. Such

men cannot be adequately identified here: the CPE samples' variable for bounties includes only federal payments, but states and localities paid their own bounties that often exceeded the federal amount. The small percentage of native-born men enlisting as substitutes includes African Americans, which is why the variable was not employed in Chapter 3.

18. See Peter Blanck, "Civil War Pensions and Disability," *Ohio State Law Journal* 62 (2001), 135–146; Glasson, *Federal Pensions*, 174–175; Theda Skocpol, *Protecting Soldiers and Mothers: The Political Origins of Social Policy in the United States* (Cambridge, MA: Harvard University Press, 1992), 116–117. It should be noted that the GAR itself was cool toward foreign-born veterans; see Stuart McConnell, *Glorious Contentment: The Grand Army of the Republic, 1865–1900* (Chapel Hill: University of North Carolina Press, 1992), 209–210.

19. Literacy among men aged thirty to fifty in the 1870 census, defined as ability to read and write (including in a non-English tongue), was found among 83.1 percent of those born in English-speaking countries, 93.7 percent born in non-English-speaking countries, and 92.3 of native-born whites. Average wealth (real and personal property combined) was $1,660 for men from English-speaking countries, $2,629 for non-native-English speakers, and $3,342 for native-born whites. These comparisons are derived from the IPUMS census samples (Steven Ruggles et al., *Integrated Public Use Microdata Series: Version 3.0* [machine-readable database] [Minneapolis: Minnesota Population Center, 2004]). Using members of the CPE samples with known death dates, the crude death rate from 1865 to 1890 was 7.66 for English-speaking immigrants, 6.65 for those from non-English-speaking countries, and 5.08 for native-born whites.

20. When Fichter applied again, his pension was reduced. Examining Surgeons' Certificates, Feb. 25, 1881, Jan. 23, 1884, File of George Fichter (9th Illinois Infantry), Pension Files.

21. Prescott F. Hall, quoted in Russell A. Kazal, *Becoming Old Stock: The Paradox of German-American Identity* (Princeton,

NJ: Princeton University Press, 2004), 122; Henry C. Merwin, "The Irish in American Life," *Atlantic Monthly*, March 1896, 289.

22. Testimony of Thomas B. Hood, in U.S. House of Representatives, Select Committee on Payment of Pensions, Bounty, and Back Pay, *Report on the Condition and Management of the Pension Bureau*, 46th Cong., 3rd sess., 578.

23. Ibid.

Chapter 5 "A More Infamous Gang of Cut-Throats Never Lived"

1. Studies that discuss pension attorneys include Peter Blanck and Chen Song, "Civil War Pension Attorneys and Disability Politics," *Journal of Law Reform* 35 (2002), 137–217; Donald R. Shaffer, *After the Glory: The Struggles of Black Civil War Veterans* (Lawrence: University Press of Kansas, 2004), 125–127; Theda Skocpol, *Protecting Soldiers and Mothers: The Political Origins of Social Policy in the United States* (Cambridge, MA: Harvard University Press, 1992), 114–118; John William Oliver, "History of the Civil War Pensions, 1861–1885," *Bulletin of the University of Wisconsin*, History Series, 4 (1915), 33–34, 49–50, 98–102; Carrie Kiewitt, "A Study of Fraud in African-American Civil War Pensions: Augustus Parlett Lloyd, Pension Attorney, 1881–1909," (M.A. thesis, University of Richmond, 1996).

2. More than 60,000 individuals were certified at one time or another to represent pension applicants; see *Report of Commissioner* [1898], 55th Cong., 35d sess., 56. On women who headed claim houses, see Jill Norgren, *Belva Lockwood: The Woman Who Would Be President* (New York: New York University Press, 2007); *New York Times*, Dec. 28, 1883. On agents' suspected collusion with the government, see ibid., March 24, 1894. Claim-house assistance appeared as an independent variable in Chapters 3 and 4 only in regard to Pension Bureau decisions. Examining physicians had no direct knowledge of assistance by claim houses, though agent coaching might have helped applicants prepare for the medical examination; however, claim-house assistance, if included as a variable in Table 3–5 (not shown), makes virtually no difference in the odds of a favorable physician-board recommendation.

3. For testimony by an attorney whose firm handled pensions and who believed that a claim agent should be required to "be a lawyer in good standing before the Federal courts in the State where he resides," see Testimony of Charles King, in U.S. House of Representatives, Select Committee on Payment of Pensions, Bounty, and Back Pay, *Report on the Condition and Management of the Pension Bureau*, 46th Cong., 3rd sess., 171–256 (quote from 171). On agents' other occupations, see *New York Times*, Nov. 21, 1883.

4. *SL*, 37th Cong., 2nd sess., 568; Oliver, "Civil War Pensions," 16, 31–34.

5. Oliver, "Civil War Pensions," 49–50.

6. *Report of Commissioner* [1883], 48th Cong., 2nd sess., 316; *National Tribune*, Aug. 27, 1881. Table 5–1 is based on claim houses listed for first-time applicants in the CPE samples. A firm's entry is estimated by the earliest application that cites it; firms occasionally took over applications that predated their formation, so Table 5–1's second column is an approximation.

7. Oliver, "Civil War Pensions," 99–102.

8. Ibid., 101–102.

9. *New York Times*, Dec. 6, 1890, Aug. 13, 1891; *SL*, 59th Cong., 2nd sess., 379.

10. A congressional committee estimated that $37 million had been paid to claim agents through 1890 (including fees for pensions to widows and other dependents), and a subsequent tally by the pension commissioner reported an additional $11.9 million in fees from 1891 through 1900; U.S. House of Representatives, Committee on Invalid Pensions, *Report on Fees in Pension Cases*, 51st Cong., 2nd sess., 2; *Report of Commissioner* [1901], 57th Cong., 1st sess., 67. On subagents, see the advertisement for "a trusty agent in each county in the Southern States to secure claims of colored soldiers, their widows, children and parents .... A live man can do a great deal of good"; *Christian Recorder*, Sept. 25, 1890. Lemon's carefully timed purchase of Nathan W. Fitzgerald's firm is summarized in Oliver, "Civil War Pensions," 100–101. Quotes from *New York Times*, Dec. 6, 1890, Dec. 16, 1897, March 24, 1894

Nov. 12, 1883; *Report of Commissioner* [1878], 45th Cong., 3rd sess., 325.

11. Quoted in *Congressional Globe*, 41st Cong., 2nd sess., 1967; Kiewitt, "African-American Civil War Pensions," 28.

12. U.S. House of Representatives, Select Committee on Payment of Pensions, Bounty, and Back Pay, *Report on the Condition and Management of the Pension Bureau,* 46th Cong., 3rd sess., 177; *Report of Commissioner* [1894], 53rd Cong., 3rd sess., 34; [John A. Logan], in Mary S. Logan, ed., *Thirty Years in Washington: Or, Life and Scenes in Our National Capital* (Hartford, CT: Worthington, 1901), 373.

13. See Chapter 3 for discussion of slave-state birth and later-life deprivation. To elaborate on that chapter's consideration of literacy as a signifier of veterans' ability to navigate bureaucratic procedures, pension applicants' ability to write was recorded erratically on their applications. Nineteen percent of applications are missing the notation on writing, with substantial biases in the omissions: 10.8 percent of black veterans' notations are missing, versus 24 percent for German immigrants, 33 percent for Irish-born immigrants, and 30 percent for other immigrants. This variable is thus unsuitable for inclusion in Table 5–4.

14. Logan, *Thirty Years in Washington*, 373.

15. *Report of Commissioner* [1905], 59th Cong., 1st sess., 530; *Report of Commissioner* [1897], 55th Cong., 2nd sess., 45. The average of 100 disqualifications is calculated from pension commissioners' reports from 1877 through 1898, the years in which suspensions, disbarments, and other disciplinary actions (by the interior secretary on the Pension Bureau's recommendation) are reported in comparable format.

16. See U.S. House of Representatives, Committee on Payment of Pensions, Bounty, and Back Pay, *Testimony on Passage of Certain Pension Laws,* 48th Cong., 2nd sess., 93–99; *New York Times*, Dec. 8, Oct. 17, 1883; Oliver, "History of Pensions," 100–101.

17. Speech by John F. Benjamin, in *Congressional Globe*, 41st Cong., 2nd sess., 1967; *New York Times*, June 20, 1893.

Chapter 6 Havens of Last Resort

1. See Patrick J. Kelly, *Creating a National Home: Building the Veterans' Welfare State, 1860–1900* (Cambridge, MA: Harvard University Press, 1997); Judith G. Cetina, "A History of Veterans' Homes in the United States: 1811–1930," (Ph.D. diss., Case Western Reserve University, 1977); Larry M. Logue, "Union Veterans and Their Government: The Effects of Public Policies on Private Lives," *Journal of Interdisciplinary History* 22 (1992), 411–434. Yearly membership figures for the federal system are given in *Managers Report* [1930], 71st Cong., 3rd sess., 50–51.

2. Kelly, *National Home*, 128, 140–154, 183–197; James Marten, "A Place of Great Beauty, Improved by Man: The Soldiers' Home and Victorian Milwaukee, Wisconsin," *Milwaukee History* 22 (1999), 2–15.

3. Kelly, *National Home*, 98–99; Donald R. Shaffer, *After the Glory: The Struggles of Black Civil War Veterans* (Lawrence: University Press of Kansas, 2004), 137–142. In 1908, the peak year of the homes' occupancy, African Americans made up 3.5 percent of residents cared for; see *Board of Managers Report* [1908], 60th Cong., 2nd sess., 8. States also operated their own soldiers' homes, receiving federal subsidies after the late 1880s; this chapter's discussion of CPE members' residence in a soldiers' home also includes state-operated homes.

4. Quoted in Kelly, *National Home*, 135.

5. It should also be noted that because sample members are followed over time in this analysis, inclusion of occupation, which one study suggested was significant in decisions to seek institutionalization (see Cetina, "Veterans' Homes," 404–406), is also infeasible since occupations consistently appear in pension documents (primarily the examining physicians' report) only after 1900. Because soldiers' homes were separate from the pension system, the tables in this chapter report veterans' actions past this study's 1907 ending date for pension analysis.

6. A similar caution about the black population at risk to enter a soldiers' home is expressed in Shaffer, *Beyond the Glory*, 138.

Soldiers' home residence was not a permanent status – residents could obtain furloughs for shorter absences or discharges if they meant to leave permanently, and many were then readmitted. Residence statistics in this chapter refer to the first-known residence in a home.

7. For a discussion of such arrangements, with particular reference to African-American pensioners, see Elizabeth A. Regosin and Donald R. Shaffer, eds., *Voices of Emancipation: Understanding Slavery, the Civil War, and Reconstruction through the U.S. Pension Bureau Files* (New York: New York University Press, 2008), 145–149; on migration of African-American veterans, see Dora L. Costa and Matthew E. Kahn, *Heroes and Cowards: The Social Face of War* (Princeton, NJ: Princeton University Press, 2008), 189–203. Interstate moves used in the rootlessness index do not include a move to a soldiers' home. The index does not address the availability of children as caregivers; although co-resident relatives are noted in the CPE data when they are mentioned in pension records, the records do not indicate if or when the coresidents left the veteran's household.

8. See Roger Daniels, *Coming to America: A History of Immigration and Ethnicity in American Life* (New York: HarperCollins, 1990), 126–145; James R. Barrett and David R. Roediger, "The Irish and the 'Americanization' of the 'New Immigrants' in the Streets and in the Churches of the Urban United States, 1900–1930," *Journal of American Ethnic History* 24 (2005), 3–33; Shaffer, *After the Glory*, 137–141. The latter study hints that African Americans may have disproportionately seen resort to soldiers' homes as unmanly, which would accord with suggestions in Chapter 3, but there is little in the CPE data to allow a further test.

9. In contrast to the low-ranking chi-squares for African Americans in Table 6–3, for example, the chi-square for Pension Bureau reviewers' use of race in decisions analyzed in Table 3–6 (not shown) ranks first among variables before 1890 and second from 1890 to 1907.

10. U.S. House of Representatives, Committee on Military Affairs, *Report on the National Asylum*, 41st Cong., 3rd sess., 68; *Managers*

Report [1875], 44th Cong., 1st sess., 3. The managers' annual reports do not provide statistics on applications for admission approved and rejected.

11. *Managers Report* [1871], 42nd Cong., 2nd sess., 5 – 6; Allen R. Foote, "Degradation by Pensions–The Protest of Loyal Volunteers," *Forum,* Dec. 1891, 28.

12. Daniel P. Carpenter, *The Forging of Bureaucratic Autonomy: Reputations, Networks, and Policy Innovation in Executive Agencies, 1862–1928* (Princeton, NJ: Princeton University Press, 2001), 50, 59–60; Theda Skocpol, *Protecting Soldiers and Mothers: The Political Origins of Social Policy in the United States* (Cambridge, MA: Harvard University Press, 1992), 118–120, 143–148.

13. See Chapter 2 for a discussion of the proposal to reform the medical-examination system. For examples of requests for Congressional action and their results, see *Report of Commissioner* [1881], 46th Cong., 3rd sess., 733–739; *Report of Commissioner* [1884], 48th Cong., 1st sess., 242–244; *Report of Commissioner* [1885], 49th Cong., 1st sess., 105–107; *Report of Commissioner* [1886], 49th Cong., 2nd sess., 647–649; *Report of Commissioner* [1893], 53rd Cong., 2nd sess., 9–15.

14. See Carpenter, *Bureaucratic Autonomy*, 83–112.

Chapter 7 Epilogue

1. Military and pension records of Hiram E. Smith (8th Connecticut Infantry), recruit's identification number 100805075; David James Thompson (1st U.S. Colored Infantry), recruit's identification number 9000106228; Samuel Guttmann (52nd New York Infantry), recruit's identification number 1305207026; in *MPM Records* and *Surgeons' Certificates.*

2. The Pension Bureau continued the practice, authorized in 1873, of instructing physicians to rate miscellaneous disabilities as fractions of $18. Hiram Smith was rated at 6/18 for heart disease plus 4/18 for rheumatism, and David Thompson at 4/18 and Samuel Guttmann at 6/18 for rheumatism. See *SL*, 42nd

Cong., 3rd sess., 569; U.S. Bureau of Pensions, *Instructions to Examining Surgeons* (Washington, D.C.: Government Printing Office, 1891), 18–21.

3. For the case alleging systemic racism, see Joe R. Feagin, *Racist America: Roots, Current Realities, and Future Reparations* (New York: Routledge, 2000).

4. K. Walter Hickel, "Medicine, Bureaucracy, and Social Welfare: The Politics of Disability Compensation for American Veterans of World War I," in Paul K. Longmore and Lauri Umansky, eds., *The New Disability History: American Perspectives* (New York: New York University Press, 2001), 236–267.

5. Ibid., 257, 258. By the early 1920s, Veterans Bureau officials were examining more than 380,000 applicants per year; ibid., 262n.

6. Robert F. Jefferson, "'Enabled Courage': Race, Disability, and Black World War II Veterans in Postwar America," *Historian* 65 (2003), 1118, 1119. Physicians performed nearly 1.8 million examinations for disability compensation in fiscal year 1946, and were still conducting more than a million examinations in fiscal 1949. See U.S. Veterans Administration, *Annual Report of Administrator of Veterans Affairs*, 80th Cong., 1st sess., 79; 81st Cong., 2nd sess., 153.

7. See Doris Zames Fleischer and Frieda Zames, *The Disability Rights Movement: From Charity to Confrontation* (Philadelphia, PA: Temple University Press, 2001); Joseph P. Shapiro, *No Pity: People with Disabilities Forging a New Civil Rights Movement* (New York: Times Books, 1993); Richard K. Scotch, *From Good Will to Civil Rights: Transforming Federal Disability Policy* (Philadelphia, PA: Temple University Press, 1984); Jacqueline Vaughn Switzer, *Disabled Rights: American Disability Policy and the Fight for Equality* (Washington, D.C.: Georgetown University Press, 2003); David A. Gerber, "Disabled Veterans, the State, and the Experience of Disability in Western Societies, 1914–1950," *Journal of Social History* 36 (2003), 899–916. Bush quoted in William N. Myhill and Peter Blanck, "Disability and Aging: Historical and Contemporary Challenges," *Elder's Advisor*, forthcoming.

8. Michelle van Ryn and Jane Burke, "The Effect of Patient Race and Socio-Economic Status on Physicians' Perception of Patients," *Social Science and Medicine* 50 (2000), 813–828; Raymond C. Tait et al., "Management of Occupational Back Injuries: Differences among African Americans and Caucasians," *Journal of Pain* 112 (2004), 389–396. See also John F. Dovidio et al., "Disparities and Distrust: The Implications of Psychological Processes for Understanding Racial Disparities in Health and Health Care," *Social Science and Medicine* 67 (2008), 478–486. For a contemporary study of organizational culture and conceptions of disability, see Lisa Schur, Douglas Kruse, Joseph Blasi, and Peter Blanck, "Is Disability Disabling In All Workplaces? Disability, Workplace Disparities, and Corporate Culture," *Industrial Relations* 48 (2009), 381–410.

9. The Pension Bureau's backlog reached 483,000 cases in 1892–93 (first-time claims only, but including widows and dependents); *Report of Commissioner* [1893], 53rd Cong., 2nd sess., 27–28. Quotes from Testimony of Ian de Planque, U.S. House of Representatives, Committee on Veterans' Affairs, Testimony before Subcommittee on Disability Assistance and Memorial Affairs, June 18, 2009, Congressional Information Service H-76–20090618; Testimony of David Cox, U.S. Senate, Committee on Veterans' Affairs, Testimony Taken July 9, 2008, *Congressional Quarterly Congressional Testimony*; Maureen Murdoch et al., "Racial Disparities in VA Service Connection for Posttraumatic Stress Disorder Disability," *Medical Care* 41 (2003), 536–549.

10. "Resources" in modern times encompass more than personnel, as one senator made clear: "We've talked about staffing, we've talked about additional money, technology, training, adjudication process, rating schedule, [but] ... we've put money, we've staffed up, still not getting much better." Statement of John Tester, Senate Veterans' Affairs Committee, July 9, 2008.

11. For details on "willful misconduct" and how it is to be interpreted, see National Archives and Records Administration, Office of Federal Register, *Code of Federal Regulations, Title 38: Pensions,*

Bonuses, and Veterans' Relief (Washington, D.C.: U.S. Government Printing Office, 2008), Sec. 3.301.

12. On recent legislation, see Peter Blanck, "'The Right to Live in the World': Disability Yesterday, Today, and Tomorrow – The 2008 Jacobus tenBroek Disability Law Symposium," *Texas Journal on Civil Liberties and Civil Rights* 13 (2008), 367–401.

Appendix

1. An excellent description of the origins and course of the project that resulted in these data is Larry T. Wimmer, "Reflections on the Early Indicators Project: A Partial History," in Dora L. Costa, ed., *Health and Labor Force Participation over the Life Cycle* (Chicago: University of Chicago Press, 2003), 1–10; see also Robert W. Fogel, "New Sources and New Techniques for the Study of Secular Trends in Nutritional Status, Health, Mortality, and the Process of Aging," *Historical Methods* 26 (1993), 5–43. The data collection project was supported by Award Number P01 AG10120 from the National Institute on Aging. The original sample design excluded commissioned officers, but the sample of white companies includes men promoted from the ranks and the U.S. Colored Troops sample includes company-level officers. This book focuses solely on enlisted men.

2. The CPE African-American sample constitutes an oversample: black recruits make up 14.7 percent of the combined white and black samples, whereas African Americans were approximately 8.4 percent of all Union recruits. On the Union total of approximately 2.1 million soldiers (some estimates include sailors as well), see *Report of Commissioner* [1882], 47th Cong., 2nd sess., 723–725; U.S. Census Bureau, *Historical Statistics of the United States, Colonial Times to 1970* (Washington, D.C.: Government Printing Office, 1975), pt. 2, 1140; James M. McPherson, *Battle Cry of Freedom: The Civil War Era* (New York: 1988), 306–307n; Benjamin A. Gould, *Investigations in the Military and Anthropological Statistics of American Soldiers* (New York: Hurd and Houghton, 1869), 27. Applying the ratio of enlistments to individuals in this

article's samples to the total enlistments given in *OR,* ser. 3, vol. 4, 1269–1270, likewise produces a total of just under 2.1 million soldiers; on the number of black soldiers, see ibid. Black veterans are weighted downward to comprise 8.4 percent of the total in tables based on combination of the black and white samples.

3. Life-table values were computed for CPE nonapplicants with known death dates, and a bellwether measure can be compared to estimates for contemporary Americans:

	CPE White	CPE Black	U.S. White Men, 1880	U.S. Black Men, 1910
Life expectancy at 20 (e_{20})	19.6	18.4	40.0	34.6

Comparison data from Michael R. Haines, "Estimated Life Tables for the United States, 1850–1910," *Historical Methods* 31 (1998), 159, 167. See also Douglas Ewbank, "History of Black Mortality and Health before 1940," *Milbank Memorial Fund Quarterly* 65 supp. 1 (1987), 100–128, which summarizes a number of studies of African-American mortality. The large disparities between CPE nonapplicants and the general life tables indicates that the former are more relevant to CPE nonapplicants without death dates.

4. For introductions to hazards analysis and its applicability to historical data, see John G. Treble, "On Marrows: Evidence from the Victorian Household Panel Study," *Historical Methods* 28 (1995), 183–193; J. Morgan Kousser, "'The Onward March of Right Principles': State Legislative Actions on Racial Discrimination in Schools in Nineteenth-Century America," *Historical Methods* 35 (2002), 177–204. For technical discussions, see Janet M. Box-Steffensmeier and Bradford S. Jones, *Event History Modeling: A Guide for Social Scientists* (New York: Cambridge University Press, 2004); Judith B. Singer and John B. Willett, *Applied Longitudinal Data Analysis: Modeling Change and Event Occurrence* (New York: Oxford University Press, 2003). A modified form of logistic regression can be used

for event analysis: see, e.g., Nathaniel Beck, "Modeling Space and Time: The Event History Approach," in Elinor Scarbrough and Eric Tanenbaum, eds., *Research Strategies in the Social Sciences* (New York: Oxford University Press, 1998), 191–216. The tie-breaking method in Table 6–3 mirrors the logistic-regression approach.

Bibliography

Primary Sources

Machine-readable data archives

Fogel, Robert W. et al. *Aging of Veterans of the Union Army: Military, Pension, and Medical Records, 1820–1940*. Chicago: University of Chicago, Center for Population Economics, 2000.

—. *Aging of Veterans of the Union Army: Surgeons' Certificates, Version S-1 Standardized, 1862–1940*. Chicago: University of Chicago, Center for Population Economics, 2000.

Ruggles, Steven et al. *Integrated Public Use Microdata Series: Version 3.0*. Minneapolis: Minnesota Population Center, 2004.

Manuscripts

National Archives, Washington, D.C. Pension Files, 1861–1934

Government Publications

Board of Managers of National Home for Disabled Volunteer Soldiers. *Annual Reports. U.S. Congressional Serial Set,* 1875–1930.

Bibliography

National Archives and Records Administration, Office of Federal Register. *Code of Federal Regulations, Title 38: Pensions, Bonuses, and Veterans' Relief.* Washington, D.C.: Government Printing Office, 2008.

U.S. Bureau of the Census. *Historical Statistics of the United States, Colonial Times to 1970.* 2 vols. Washington, D.C.: Government Printing Office, 1975.

U.S. Congress. *Congressional Globe.*

—. *Congressional Record.*

—. *U.S. Statutes at Large.*

U.S. Department of Interior. *Annual Report. U.S. Congressional Serial Set,* 52nd Cong., 1st sess.

U.S.Department of Interior, Bureau of Pensions. *Reports of Commissioner of Pensions. U.S. Congressional Serial Set,* 41st-59th Cong.

—. *General Instructions to Special Examiners of the United States Pension Office.* Washington, D.C.: Government Printing Office, 1881.

—. *Instructions to Examining Surgeons.* Washington, D.C.: Government Printing Office, 1873–1895.

—. *Treatise on the Practice of the Pension Bureau.* Washington, D.C.: Government Printing Office, 1898.

U.S. House of Representatives, Committee on Invalid Pensions. *Report on Fees in Pension Cases. U.S. Congressional Serial* Set, 51st Cong., 2nd sess.

U.S. House of Representatives, Committee on Military Affairs. *Report on the National Asylum. U.S. Congressional Serial Set,* 41st Cong., 3rd sess.

U.S. House of Representatives, Committee on Payment of Pensions, Bounty, and Back Pay. *Report on the Condition and Management of the Pension Bureau. U.S. Congressional Serial Set,* 46th Cong., 3rd sess.

—. *Testimony on Passage of Certain Pension Laws. U.S. Congressional Serial Set,* 48th Cong., 2nd sess.

U.S.House of Representatives, Committee on Veterans' Affairs. Testimony before Subcommittee on Disability Assistance and

Memorial Affairs, June 18, 2009. Congressional Information Service H-76–20090618.

U.S. House of Representatives, Select Committee on Charges against the Commissioner of Pensions. *Report on Management of the Bureau of Pensions. U.S. Congressional Serial Set,* 51st Cong., 2nd sess.

U.S. Senate, Committee on Appropriations. *Estimates of Claims of Colored Soldiers and Sailors. U.S. Congressional Serial Set,* 45th Cong., 2nd sess.

U.S. Senate, Committee on Pensions. Letter from Secretary of Interior to Committee on Pensions. *U.S. Congressional Serial Set,* 45th Cong., 2nd sess.

U.S. Senate, Committee on Veterans ' Affairs. Testimony taken July 9, 2008. *Congressional Quarterly Congressional Testimony.*

U.S. Surgeon General' s Office. *Medical and Surgical History of the Civil War.* 15 vols. Wilmington, N.C.: Broadfoot, 1990–1992 (orig. pub. 1870–1888).

U.S. Veterans Administration. *Annual Reports of Administrator of Veterans Affairs. U.S. Congressional Serial Set,* 1946–1949.

U.S. War Department. *Revised Regulations for the Army of the United States, 1861.* Philadelphia: George W. Childs, 1862.

—. *War of the Rebellion: A Compilation of the Official Records of the Union and Confederate Armies, 1861–1865.* 127 vols. Washington, D.C.: Government Printing Office, 1880–1901.

Books and Articles

Bartlett, Asa W. *History of the Twelfth Regiment, New Hampshire Volunteers in the War of the Rebellion.* Concord, NH: Ira C. Evans, 1897.

Bentham, Jeremy. "Situation and Relief of the Poor." In John Bowring, comp., *The Works of Jeremy Bentham.* Edinburgh: William Tait, 1843, 8: 361–362.

Billings, John D. *Hardtack and Coffee.* Boston, MA: G. M. Smith, 1887.

Bibliography

Britton, Wiley. *A Traveling Court: Based on the Investigation of War Claims.* Kansas City, MO: Smith-Grieves, 1926.

Casselman, A. B. "An Inside View of the Pension Bureau." *Century*, May 1893, 135–140.

Foote, Allen R. "Degradation by Pensions – The Protest of Loyal Volunteers." *Forum*, Dec. 1891, 427–428.

Gould, Benjamin A. *Investigations in the Military and Anthropological Statistics of American Soldiers.* New York: Hurd and Houghton, 1869.

Hess, Earl J., ed. *A German in the Yankee Fatherland: The Civil War Letters of Henry A. Kircher.* Kent, OH: Kent State University Press, 1983.

Hoffman, Frederick L. "The Race Traits and Tendencies of the American Negro." *Publications of the American Economic Association* 11 (1896), 1–329.

Logan, Mary S., ed. *Thirty Years in Washington: Or, Life and Scenes in Our National Capital.* Hartford, CT: Worthington, 1901.

Merwin, Henry C. "The Irish in American Life." *Atlantic Monthly*, March 1896, 289–301.

New General English Dictionary. London: Topis and Bunney, 1781.

Ross, Edward A. *The Old World in the New: The Significance of Past and Present Immigration to the American People.* New York: Century, 1914.

Sloane, William M. "Pensions and Socialism." *Century,* June 1891, 179–189.

Walker, Francis A. "Restriction of Immigration." *Atlantic Monthly*, June 1896, 822–829.

Newspapers

Christian Recorder

National Tribune

New York Times

Secondary Sources

Books

Allendorf, Donald. *Long Road to Liberty: The Odyssey of a German Regiment in the Yankee Army.* Kent, OH: Kent State University Press, 2006.

Ayers, Edward L. *The Promise of the New South: Life after Reconstruction.* New York: Oxford University Press, 1992.

Bacarella, Michael. *Lincoln's Foreign Legion: The 39th New York Infantry, the Garibaldi Guard.* Shippensburg, PA: White Mane, 1996.

Bay, Mia. *The White Image in the Black Mind: African-American Ideas about White People. 1830–1925.* New York: Oxford University Press, 2000.

Baynton, Douglas C. *Forbidden Signs: American Culture and the Campaign against Sign Language.* Chicago, IL: University of Chicago Press, 1996.

Bederman, Gail. *Manliness and Civilization: A Cultural History of Gender and Race in the United States, 1880–1917.* Chicago, IL: University of Chicago Press, 1995.

Berry, Mary Frances. *My Face Is Black Is True: Callie House and the Struggle for Ex-Slave Reparations.* New York: Knopf, 2005.

Bilby, Joseph G. *Remember Fontenoy! The 69th New York and the Irish Brigade in the Civil War.* Hightstown, NJ: Longstreet House, 1995.

Blanck, Peter, Eve Hill, Charles Siegal, and Michael Waterstone, eds. *Disability Civil Rights Law and Policy: Cases and Materials.* St. Paul, MN: Thomson/West, 2009.

Box-Steffensmeier, Janet M., and Bradford S. Jones. *Event History Modeling: Guide for Social Scientists.* New York: Cambridge University Press, 2004.

Bruce, Susannah U. *The Harp and the Eagle: Irish-American Volunteers and the Union Army, 1861–1865.* New York: New York University Press, 2006.

Burchard, Peter. *One Gallant Rush: Robert Gould Shaw and His Brave Black Regiment.* New York: St. Martin's, 1965.

Bibliography

Burton, William L. *Melting Pot Soldiers: The Union's Ethnic Regiments.* Ames, IA: Iowa State University Press, 1988.

Byrd, W. Michael, and Linda A. Clayton. *An American Health Dilemma: A Medical History of African Americans and the Problem of Race.* 2 vols. New York: Routledge, 2000.

Carpenter, Daniel P. *The Forging of Bureaucratic Autonomy: Reputations, Networks, and Policy Innovation in Executive Agencies, 1862–1928.* Princeton, NJ: Princeton University Press, 2001.

Costa, Dora L., and Matthew E. Kahn. *Heroes and Cowards: The Social Face of War.* Princeton, NJ: Princeton University Press, 2008.

Daniels, Roger. *Coming to America: A History of Immigration and Ethnicity in American Life.* New York: HarperCollins, 1990.

Davis, Lennard J. *Enforcing Normalcy: Disability, Deafness, and the Body.* London: Verso, 1995.

Dean, Jr., Eric T. *Shook over Hell: Post-Traumatic Stress, Vietnam, and the Civil War.* Cambridge, MA: Harvard University Press, 1997.

Dearing, Mary R. *Veterans in Politics: The Story of the G.A.R.* Baton Rouge: Louisiana State University Press, 1952.

Engle, Stephen D. *The Yankee Dutchman: The Life of Franz Sigel.* Fayetteville: University of Arkansas Press, 1993.

Feagin, Joe R. *Racist America: Roots, Current Realities, and Future Reparations.* New York: Routledge, 2000.

Fleischer, Doris Zames, and Frieda Zames. *The Disability Rights Movement: From Charity to Confrontation.* Philadelphia, PA: Temple University Press, 2001.

Foster, Roy, John M. Hearne, and Rory T. Cornish, eds. *Thomas Francis Meagher: The Making of an Irish American.* Portland, OR: Irish Academic Press, 2005.

Fredrickson, George M. *The Black Image in the White Mind: The Debate on Afro-American Character and Destiny, 1817–1914.* New York: Harper, Row, 1971.

Garland-Thompson, Rosemarie. *Staring: How We Look.* New York: Oxford University Press, 2009.

Gerber, David A., ed. *Disabled Veterans in History*. Ann Arbor: University of Michigan Press, 2000.

Gilmore, Glenda. *Gender and Jim Crow: Women and the Politics of White Supremacy in North Carolina, 1896–1920*. Chapel Hill: University of North Carolina Press, 1996.

Glasson, William H. *Federal Military Pensions in the United States*. New York: Oxford University Press, 1918.

Glatthaar, Joseph T. *Forged in Battle: The Civil War Alliance of Black Soldiers and White Officers*. New York: Free Press, 1990.

Goffman, Erving. *Stigma: Notes on the Management of Spoiled Identity*. Englewood Cliffs, NJ: Prentice-Hall, 1963.

Grob, Gerald N. *The Deadly Truth: A History of Disease in America*. Cambridge, MA: Harvard University Press, 2002.

—. *The Mad among Us: A History of the Care of America's Mentally Ill*. New York: Free Press, 1994.

Guterl, Matthew Pratt. *The Color of Race in America, 1900–1940*. Cambridge, MA: Harvard University Press, 2001.

Higham, John. *Strangers in the Land: Patterns in American Nativism, 1860–1925*. New Brunswick, NJ: Rutgers University Press, 1955.

Jacobson, Matthew Frye. *Whiteness of a Different Color: European Immigrants and the Alchemy of Race*. Cambridge, MA: Harvard University Press, 1998.

Jordan, Winthrop D. *White over Black: American Attitudes toward the Negro, 1550–1812*. Chapel Hill: University of North Carolina Press, 1968.

Kazal, Russell A. *Becoming Old Stock: The Paradox of German-American Identity*. Princeton, NJ: Princeton University Press, 2004.

Kelly, Patrick J. *Creating a National Home: Building the Veterans' Welfare State, 1860–1900*. Cambridge, MA: Harvard University Press, 1997.

Kiple, Kenneth F., and Virginia H. King. *Another Dimension to the Black Diaspora: Diet, Disease, and Racism*. New York: Cambridge University Press, 1981.

Levine, Peter. *Ellis Island to Ebbets Field: Sport and the American Jewish Experience*. New York: Oxford University Press, 1992.

Bibliography

Lonn, Ella. *Foreigners in the Union Army and Navy*. Baton Rouge: Louisiana State University Press, 1951.

McConnell, Stuart. *Glorious Contentment: The Grand Army of the Republic, 1865–1900*. Chapel Hill: University of North Carolina Press, 1992.

McPherson, James M. *Battle Cry of Freedom: The Civil War Era*. New York: Oxford University Press, 1988.

Mahin, Dean B. *The Blessed Place of Freedom: Europeans in Civil War America*. Washington, D.C.: Brassey's, 2002.

Medley, Audrey. *Race in North America: Origin and Evolution of a Worldview*. Boulder, CO: Westview, 1993.

Nevels, Cynthia Skove. *Lynching to Belong: Claiming Whiteness through Racial Violence*. College Station: Texas A&M University Press, 2007.

Norgren, Jill. *Belva Lockwood: The Woman Who Would Be President*. New York: New York University Press, 2007.

Orloff, Ann Shola. *The Politics of Pensions: A Comparative Analysis of Britain, Canada, and the United States, 1880–1940*. Madison: University of Wisconsin Press, 1993.

Preston, Samuel H., and Michael R. Haines. *Fatal Years: Child Mortality in Late Nineteenth-Century America*. Princeton, NJ: Princeton University Press, 1991.

Pula, James S. *The Sigel Regiment: History of the 26th Wisconsin Volunteer Infantry, 1862–1865*. Campbell, CA: Savas, 1998.

Regosin, Elizabeth A. *Freedom's Promise: Ex-Slave Families and Citizenship in the Age of Emancipation*. Charlottesville: University Press of Virginia, 2002.

Regosin, Elizabeth A., and Donald R. Shaffer, eds. *Voices of Emancipation: Understanding Slavery, the Civil War, and Reconstruction through the U.S. Pension Bureau Files*. New York: New York University Press, 2008.

Resch, John P. *Suffering Soldiers: Revolutionary War Veterans, Moral Sentiment, and Political Culture in the Early Republic*. Amherst: University of Massachusetts Press, 1999.

Roediger, David. *The Wages of Whiteness: Race and the Making of the American Working Class*. London: Verso, 1991.

Rothman, David J. *The Discovery of the Asylum: Social Order and Disorder in the New Republic.* Boston, MA: Little, Brown, 1971.

Schweik, Susan. *The Ugly Laws: Disability in Public.* New York: New York University Press, 2009.

Scotch, Richard K. *From Good Will to Civil Rights: Transforming Federal Disability Policy.* Philadelphia, PA: Temple University Press, 1984.

Sears, Stephen W. *Chancellorsville.* Boston, MA: Houghton Mifflin, 1996.

Shaffer, Donald R. *After the Glory: The Struggles of Black Civil War Veterans.* Lawrence: University Press of Kansas, 2004.

Shapiro, Joseph P. *No Pity: People with Disabilities Forging a New Civil Rights Movement.* New York: Times Books, 1993.

Singer, Judith B., and John B. Willett. *Applied Longitudinal Data Analysis: Modeling Change and Event Occurrence.* New York: Oxford University Press, 2003.

Skocpol, Theda. *Protecting Soldiers and Mothers: The Political Origins of Social Policy in the United States.* Cambridge, MA: Harvard University Press, 1992.

Smith, Rogers M. *Civic Ideals: Conflicting Visions of Citizenship in U.S. History.* New Haven, CT: Yale University Press, 1997.

Switzer, Jacqueline Vaughn. *Disabled Rights: American Disability Policy and the Fight for Equality.* Washington, D.C.: Georgetown University Press, 2003.

Trefousse, Hans L. *Carl Schurz: A Biography.* New York: Fordham University Press, 1998.

Valuska, David L., and Christian B. Keller, eds. *Damn Dutch: Pennsylvania Germans at Gettysburg.* Mechanicsburg, PA: Stackpole, 2004.

Webb, Sidney, and Beatrice Webb. *English Poor Law Policy.* London: Longman's, 1910.

White, Leonard D. *The Republican Era, 1869–1901: A Study in Administrative History.* Chicago: University of Chicago Press, 1958.

Wiley, Bell I. *The Life of Billy Yank: The Common Soldier of the Union.* Indianapolis: Bobbs-Merrill, 1952.

Bibliography

Articles and Chapters

Barrett, James R., and David R. Roediger. "The Irish and the 'Americanization' of the 'New Immigrants' in the Streets and in the Churches of the Urban United States, 1900–1930." *Journal of American Ethnic History* 24 (2005), 3–33.

Baynton, Douglas C. "Defectives in the Land: Disability and American Immigration Policy, 1882–1924." *Journal of American Ethnic History* 24 (2005), 31–44.

Beck, Nathaniel. "Modeling Space and Time: The Event History Approach." In Elinor Scarbrough and Eric Tanenbaum, eds., *Research Strategies in the Social Sciences*, 191–216. New York: Oxford University Press, 1998.

Black, Andrew K. "In the Service of the United States: Comparative Mortality among African-American and White Troops in the Union Army." *Journal of Negro History* 79 (1994), 317–333.

Blanck, Peter. "Civil War Pensions and Disability." *Ohio State Law Journal* 62 (2001), 109–238.

—. "'The Right to Live in the World': Disability Yesterday, Today, and Tomorrow – The 2008 Jacobus tenBroek Disability Law Symposium." *Texas Journal on Civil Liberties and Civil Rights* 13 (2008), 367–401.

Blanck, Peter, and Michael Millender. "Before Disability Civil Rights: Civil War Pensions and the Politics of Disability in America." *Alabama Law Review* 52 (2000), 1–50.

Blanck, Peter, and Chen Song. "With Malice toward None, with Charity toward All: Civil War Pensions for Native and Foreign-Born Union Army Veterans." *Transnational Law and Contemporary Problems* 11 (2001), 1–75.

—. "Civil War Pension Attorneys and Disability Politics." *Michigan Journal of Law Reform* 35 (2002), 137–217.

Burch, Susan. "Reading between the Signs: Defending Deaf Culture in Early Twentieth-Century America." In Paul K. Longmore and Lauri Umansky, eds., *The New Disability History: American Perspectives*, 214–235. New York: New York University Press, 2001.

Burch, Susan, and Ian Sutherland. "Who's Not Yet Here? American Disability History." *Radical History Review* 94 (2006), 127–147.

Clarke, Frances. "'Honorable Scars': Northern Amputees and the Meaning of Civil War Injuries." In Paul A. Cimbala and Randall Miller, eds., *Union Soldiers and the Northern Home Front: Wartime Experiences, Postwar Adjustments,* 361–394. New York: Fordham University Press, 2002.

Costa, Dora L., and Matthew E. Kahn. "Forging a New Identity: The Costs and Benefits of Diversity in Civil War Combat Units for Black Slaves and Freemen." *Journal of Economic History* 66 (2006), 936–962.

Craig, Warren A. "'Oh, God, What a Pity!' The Irish Brigade at Fredericksburg and the Creation of Myth." *Civil War History* 47 (2001), 193–221.

Crossley, Mary. "The Disability Kaleidoscope." *Notre Dame Law Review* 74 (1999), 649–660.

Dovidio, John F., Louis A. Penner, Terrance L. Albrecht, Wynne E. Norton, Samuel L. Gaertner, and J. Nicole Shelton. "Disparities and Distrust: The Implications of Psychological Processes for Understanding Racial Disparities in Health and Health Care." *Social Science and Medicine* 67 (2008), 478–486.

Ewbank, Douglas. "History of Black Mortality and Health before 1940." *Milbank Memorial Fund Quarterly* 65 supp. 1 (1987), 100–128.

Fields, Barbara Jeanne. "Ideology and Race in American History." In J. Morgan Kousser and James M. McPherson, eds., *Region, Race, and Reconstruction: Essays in Honor of C. Vann Woodward,* 143–177. New York: Oxford University Press, 1982.

Figg, Laurann, and Jane Farrell-Beck. "Amputation in the Civil War: Physical and Social Dimensions." *Journal of the History of Medicine* 48 (1993), 454–475.

Fogel, Robert W. "New Sources and New Techniques for the Study of Secular Trends in Nutritional Status, Health, Mortality, and the Process of Aging." *Historical Methods* 26 (1993), 5–43.

Furstenberg, François. "Beyond Freedom and Slavery: Autonomy, Virtue, and Resistance in Early American Political Discourse." *Journal of American History* 89 (2003), 1295–1330.

Bibliography

Galusca, Roxana. "From Fictive Ability to National Identity: Disability, Medical Inspection, and Public Health Regulations on Ellis Island." *Cultural Critique* 72 (2009), 137–163.

Gerber, David A. "Disabled Veterans, the State, and the Experience of Disability in Western Societies, 1914–1950." *Journal of Social History* 36 (2003), 899–916.

Haines, Michael R. "Estimated Life Tables for the United States, 1850–1910." *Historical Methods* 31 (1998), 149–169.

—. "The Urban Mortality Transition in the United States, 1800 to 1940." *Annales de Démographie Historique* (2001), 33–64.

Hickel, K. Walter. "Medicine, Bureaucracy, and Social Welfare: The Politics of Disability Compensation for American Veterans of World War I." In Paul K. Longmore and Lauri Umansky, eds., *The New Disability History: American Perspectives*, 236–267. New York: New York University Press, 2001.

Higham, John. "Instead of a Sequel, or How I Lost My Subject." *Reviews in American History* 28 (2000), 327–339.

Jefferson, Robert F. "'Enabled Courage': Race, Disability, and Black World War II Veterans in Postwar America." *Historian* 65 (2003), 1102–1124.

Keller, Christian B. "Pennsylvania and Virginia Germans during the Civil War: Brief History and Comparative Analysis." *Virginia Magazine of History and Biography* 109 (2001), 37–86.

Kousser, J. Morgan. "'The Onward March of Right Principles': State Legislative Actions on Racial Discrimination in Schools in Nineteenth-Century America." *Historical Methods* 35 (2002), 177–204.

Kudlick, Catherine J. "Disability History: Why We Need Another 'Other.'" *American Historical Review* 108 (2003), 763–793.

Kynoch, Gary. "Terrible Dilemmas: Black Enlistment in the Union Army during the American Civil War." *Slavery and Abolition* 18 (1997), 104–127.

Logue, Larry M. "Union Veterans and Their Government: The Effects of Public Policies on Private Lives." *Journal of Interdisciplinary History* 22 (1992), 411–434.

Logue, Larry M., and Peter Blanck. "'There Is Nothing That Promotes Longevity Like a Pension': Disability Policy and Mortality of Civil War Union Army Veterans." *Wake Forest Law Review* 39 (2004), 49–67.

—. "'Benefit of the Doubt': African American Civil War Veterans and Pensions." *Journal of Interdisciplinary History* 38 (2008), 377–397.

Longmore, Paul K., and Paul Steven Miller. "'Philosophy of Handicap': The Origins of Randolph Bourne's Radicalism." *Radical History Review* 94 (2006), 59–83.

McClintock, Megan J. "Civil War Pensions and the Reconstruction of Union Families." *Journal of American History* 83 (1996), 456–480.

McKeown, Adam. "Ritualization of Regulation: The Enforcement of Chinese Exclusion in the United States and China." *American Historical Review* 108 (2003), 377–403.

McMurry, Donald L. "The Political Significance of the Pension Question, 1885–1897." *Mississippi Valley Historical Review* 9 (1922), 19–36.

—. "The Bureau of Pensions during the Administration of President Harrison." *Mississippi Valley Historical Review* 13 (1926), 343–364.

Marten, James. "A Place of Great Beauty, Improved by Man: The Soldiers' Home and Victorian Milwaukee, Wisconsin." *Milwaukee History* 22 (1999), 2–15.

Murdoch, Maureen, James Hodges, Diane Cowper, Larry Fortner, and Michelle van Ryn. "Racial Disparities in VA Service Connection for Posttraumatic Stress Disorder Disability." *Medical Care* 41 (2003), 536–549.

Myhill, William N., and Peter Blanck. "Disability and Aging: Historical and Contemporary Challenges." *Elder's Advisor*, forthcoming.

Oliver, John W. "History of the Civil War Pensions, 1861–1885." *Bulletin of the University of Wisconsin*, History Series, 4 (1915), 1–120.

Phelan, Jo C., Bruce G. Link, and John F. Dovidio. "Stigma and Prejudice: One Animal or Two?" *Social Science and Medicine* 67 (2008), 358–367.

Bibliography

Robertson, William Glenn. "From the Crater to New Market Heights." In John David Smith, ed., *Black Soldiers in Blue: African American Troops in the Civil War Era*, 169–199. Chapel Hill: University of North Carolina Press, 2002.

Rosenberg, Charles E. "Body and Mind in Nineteenth-Century Medicine: Some Clinical Origins of the Neurosis Construct." *Bulletin of the History of Medicine* 63 (1989), 185–197.

Schur, Lisa, Douglas Kruse, Joseph Blasi, and Peter Blanck. "Is Disability Disabling In All Workplaces? Disability, Workplace Disparities, and Corporate Culture." *Industrial Relations* 48 (2009), 381–410.

Schwartzberg, Beverly. "'Lots of Them Did That': Desertion, Bigamy, and Marital Fluidity in Late-Nineteenth-Century America." *Journal of Social History* 37 (2004), 573–600.

Scott, Joan Wallach. "Gender as a Useful Category of Historical Analysis." *American Historical Review* 91 (1986), 1053–1075.

Smith, Daniel Scott. "Seasoning, Disease Environment, and Conditions of Exposure: New York Union Army Regiments and Soldiers." In Dora L. Costa, ed., *Health and Labor Force Participation over the Life Cycle*, 89–112. Chicago: University of Chicago Press, 2003.

Smith, John David. "Let Us All Be Grateful That We Have Colored Troops That Will Fight." In John David Smith, ed., *Black Soldiers in Blue: African American Troops in the Civil War Era*, 1–106. Chapel Hill: University of North Carolina Press, 2002.

Song, Chen, and Louis L. Nguyen. "The Effect of Hernias on the Labor Force Participation of Union Army Veterans." In Dora L. Costa, ed., *Health and Labor Force Participation over the Life Cycle*, 253–310. Chicago: University of Chicago Press, 2003.

Tait, Raymond C., John T. Chibnall, Elena M. Anderson, and Nortin M. Hadler. "Management of Occupational Back Injuries: Differences among African Americans and Caucasians." *Journal of Pain* 112 (2004), 389–396.

Treble, John G. "On Marrows: Evidence from the Victorian Household Panel Study." *Historical Methods* 28 (1995), 183–193.

Van Ryn, Michelle, and Jane Burke. "The Effect of Patient Race and Socio-Economic Status on Physicians' Perception of Patients." *Social Science and Medicine* 50 (2000), 813–828.

Vinovksis, Maris A. "Have Social Historians Lost the Civil War? Some Preliminary Demographic Speculations." *Journal of American History* 76 (1989), 34–58.

Waterstone, Michael, and Michael Stein. "Disabling Prejudice." *Northwestern University Law Review,* forthcoming.

West, Elliott. "Reconstructing Race." *Western Historical Quarterly* 34 (2003), 7–26.

Williams-Searle, John. "Cold Comfort: Manhood, Brotherhood, and the Transformation of Disability, 1870–1900." In Paul K. Longmore and Lauri Umansky, eds., *The New Disability History: American Perspectives,* 157–186. New York: New York University Press, 2001.

Wimmer, Larry T. "Reflections on the Early Indicators Project: Partial History." In Dora L. Costa, ed., *Health and Labor Force Participation over the Life Cycle,* 1–10. Chicago: University of Chicago Press, 2003.

Zecker, Robert M. "'Negrov Lyncovanie' and the Unbearable Whiteness of Slovaks: The Immigrant Press Covers Race." *American Studies* 43 (2002), 43–72.

Conference Presentations, Working Papers, Dissertations, and Theses

Blanck, Peter, and Chen Song. "Civil War Pensions for Union Army Veterans: Race and Disability." Paper presented at National Bureau of Economic Research Cohort Studies Meeting, 2004.

Cetina, Judith G. "History of Veterans' Homes in the United States: 1811–1930." Ph.D. diss., Case Western Reserve University, 1977.

Costa, Dora L. "Race and Older Age Mortality: Evidence from Union Army Veterans." National Bureau of Economic Research Working Paper 10902, 2004.

Evans, Richard W. "Integration of the Surgeon's Certificates with the Pension Application Groupings in the Union Army Dataset."

Working Paper, Center for Population Economics, University of Chicago, 2003.

Finocchiaro, Charles J. "Credit Claiming, Party Politics, and the Rise of Legislative Entrepreneurship in the Postbellum Congress." Paper presented at annual meeting of American Political Science Association, 2007.

—. "Constituent Service, Agency Decision Making, and Legislative Influence on the Bureaucracy in the Post Civil War Era." Paper presented at History of Congress Conference, Washington, D.C., May 2008.

Kiewitt, Carrie. "A Study of Fraud in African-American Civil War Pensions: Augustus Parlett Lloyd, Pension Attorney, 1881–1909." M.A. thesis, University of Richmond, 1996.

Salm, Martin. "The Effect of Pensions on Longevity: Evidence from Union Army Veterans." Discussion Paper No. 2668, Institute for the Study of Labor, Bonn, Germany, 2007.

Index

African Americans: in Civil War, 17, 21, 43–48; freeborn, 50, 52; freedmen, 49, 50, 52, 54–55, 122–124, 127; skin color and pensions, 58, 61, 63, 65, 69–70; treatment in Civil War pension system, 43, 56–73, 147; treatment in later pension systems, 150–152; willingness to apply for pensions, 42–43, 48–56

American Protective Association, 13

Americans with Disabilities Act (ADA), 151, 153

Ballard, Clay, 42–43, 55–56, 57, 61, 79, 81

Ballard, Mary, 42, 43

Battery Wagner, Battle of, 45

Bickford, Nathan, 118

Bourne, Randolph, 14–15

Bureau of Immigration, 34–36

Bush, George H. W., 151

Center for Population Economics (University of Chicago), 47

Chancellorsville, Battle of, 85–86, 89

Claim houses, 7, 37, 55, 67, 69, 75, 112–113, 114–117. *See also* Pension attorneys

Cleveland, Grover, 24, 28, 29, 62, 69

Crater, Battle of, 45

Death dates, estimation of, 156–157

Disability: in African-American pension applications, 73–79; as concept, 9–10, 15, 37–38; "cures" for, 2, 11–12, 19; deafness, 12; and immigration, 13–14; medical model of, 1–2, 18–19; mental illness, 11, 60, 61, 68, 73, 105–107, 148; in pension applications by foreign-born veterans, 105–107; as "prestige symbol," 3–4; social model of, 2, 18; stigmatization of, 2–6, 60

Disease during Civil War: African Americans and, 46–48, 73; foreign-born soldiers and, 89–92

Diseases in pension applications: by African Americans, 73–78; by foreign-born veterans, 105

Douglas, Stephen A., 11

Index